# Great Passenger Ships of the World

## Volume 5: 1951–1976

*Queen Elizabeth 2*

# Great Passenger Ships of the World

## Volume 5: 1951–1976

Arnold Kludas

Translated by Charles Hodges

Patrick Stephens, Wellingborough

First published in Germany under the title *Die Grossen
Passagierschiffe der Welt*
*First published in Great Britain—1977*
*Reprinted March 1986*

*British Library Cataloguing in Publication Data*

Kludas, Arnold
    Great passenger ships of the world.
    Vol. 5
    1. Passenger ships—History—Pictorial works
    I. Title    II. Die grossen Passagierschiffe
    der Welt. *English*
    387.2'43'09034    VM381

ISBN 0-85059-265-8

*Patrick Stephens Limited is part of the
Thorsons Publishing Group*

Text filmset in 10 on 12 pt English 49 by Stevenage
Printing Limited, Stevenage. Printed in Great Britain
on 100 gsm Fineblade coated cartridge, and bound, by
The Garden City Press, Letchworth, Herts, for the
publishers Patrick Stephens Limited, Denington Estate,
Wellingborough, Northants, NN8 2QD, England.

# Foreword

This fifth volume in the series takes the story of the development of large passenger ships up to the present day. During the '50s large passenger ships were once again built for regular timetabled services on all the traditional routes. At the end of that decade, however, by which time it must have become clear to even the most persistent doubter that the aeroplane was taking the dominant role in overseas passenger-carrying, orders for passenger liners were showing a marked decrease everywhere. While almost 100 passenger ships of over 10,000 GRT were launched during the '50s, the total for the decade 1961-1970 was a mere 42 units. But from the mid '60s most of the large passenger ships, then being increasingly ordered, were conceived as cruise liners. More recently the ever-growing mobility of people from the highly-developed nations has created a demand for car ferries, now often exceeding 10,000 GRT.

The present situation shows that the era of passenger ships has by no means ended, despite the forecasts of only a few years ago. On the contrary, while some 100 large passenger ships were built during the '50s and only 42 during the '60s, the curve rises sharply again for the early '70s. From 1971 up to the end of 1976 no less than 50 large passenger vessels were either launched or ordered, most of them, however, before the end of 1973, when the 'oil crisis' led to a drastic reduction in orders for new passenger ships. Nevertheless passenger services on the traditional routes continue to decrease in importance, the principal ones now being centred on Africa, Asia and the Pacific. The cruise ship occupies the centre of the stage today and is likely to continue to do so in the future. At the same time, when one considers the increasing affluence of our age, it seems that the car ferry with its often luxurious passenger accommodation has a future even on longer routes, and this might lead under certain circumstances to a renaissance in overseas liner services.

Work on this series often became rather involved, particularly the task of keeping Volume 5 up to date. This English translation of course is of the second German edition of Volume 5 (published in January 1976) and I have tried also to update it as far as possible to the time of going to press. The great pleasure which the work has nevertheless given me has been in no small way due to the helpful participation of friends, colleagues and, last but not least, people in all parts of the world, whom I had never known previously, who have sent me photographs and information quite of their own accord.

Once more, I should like to thank very sincerely all those whose valuable support I have already mentioned in my opening notes to Volumes 1-4 and who have assisted me again with this volume. And finally I should like to express once more my very deep gratitude, for their kindness in letting me use their photographs, to all those people, firms and institutions whose names appear in the Forewords and Acknowledgements to each volume. I am also pleased to say that, in conjunction with my German and British publishers, I am now preparing an additional sixth volume in this series, covering the more important 19th Century vessels of less than 10,000 GRT.

Arnold Kludas
Bremerhaven: January, 1977.

# Explanatory Notes

All passenger ships ever launched having a gross registered tonnage (GRT) of over 10,000 are presented in the five volumes of this work. This fifth volume deals with the period 1951 to 1976. The ships are arranged chronologically, with the exception of sister ships or groups of ships which have been placed together regardless of exact chronology. The chronological order of the individual sections has been determined from the launching date of the first ship of the class or group. The technical/historical biography of each ship appears under the name with which the ship first entered service. This applies also if the ship sailed later under other names and for other shipping companies. This rule is departed from only in exceptional circumstances. To trace a particular ship the reader is recommended to use the Index of Ships' Names, pages 214/226. In cases where ships have been renamed these are included after the first name in each case, as a further help in tracing all the later names, each with the year of the name change. The following is a guide to the technical and historical information concerning the ships.

## I. Technical Data

The information given in the paragraph on technical data applies fundamentally to the date when the ship first went into service as a passenger carrier. Planned specifications are given in the case of incompleted ships for which at their respective stages of construction these had not been fully decided upon. Alterations affecting technical data are noted with historical notes against the appropriate dates.

**Dimensions** Length overall × moulded breadth in metres rounded off to one place of decimals, followed by the equivalent in feet, the length to the nearest whole number and breadth to one place of decimals.

**Propulsion** Type of machinery, constructor. Where the shipbuilder has not been responsible for the propelling machinery, its constructor is given. The abbreviations III or IV exp eng indicate triple or quadruple expansion (steam) engines. In the case of passenger carrying motorships in recent years the hitherto customary large diesel engines running at low revolutions have been almost completely replaced by engines running at medium speed. This latter form of drive is described as "geared diesel".

**Power** The figure of horse power given is the highest performance attainable by the engines in normal service. The different methods of measuring horse power, according to the form of propulsion, are as follows:
IHP = indicated horse power, unit of measurement for reciprocating steam engines and internal combustion engines.
SHP = shaft horse power, unit of measurement for turbine machinery and internal combustion engines.
BHP = brake horse power, unit of measurement for internal combustion engines.
The horse power figures, thus arrived at through different methods, cannot necessarily be compared with each other. While BHP and SHP are practically identical, their relationship to the indicated horse power (IHP) is in the region of 4:5. 8,000 SHP is thus equivalent to 10,000 IHP.

**Speed** Service speed is given in knots. This is followed, as far as can be established, by the highest speed achieved on trials with the engines running at maximum power.

**Passengers** On nearly all ships the passenger accommodation and the number of berths for each class were frequently altered. Even if it were still possible today to establish all these changes exactly, the necessary effort would not justify the value of the figures thus obtained. One can come to completely different conclusions however correct the figures, for sofa-berths or emergency beds may or may not have been included. The information on alterations to passenger accommodation therefore is limited to really significant modifications, as far as it has been possible to determine them.

**Crew** Crew-strength also was subject to alteration, as for instance when a ship was converted from coal to oil-firing, or when the passenger capacity was changed. Changes in crew-strength have not been noted. Unfortunately it has not been possible to determine crew-strength for every ship.

## II. Historical Data

The historical information reflects in chronological order the career of the ship, giving all important events and facts.
Where no final fate is given for a ship (for example, sunk, broken up, etc.) it can reasonably be assumed that the vessel is still (December 1976) in the service of the last-named owners.

**Owners** In the ships' biographies, shipowners are indicated throughout by what are considered to be the accepted short-forms in English-speaking countries. Nevertheless, a selected short-form may not itself be based on an English translation of a non-English title, for instance: Nippon Yusen KK, CGT, etc. It is assumed that Cie, Cia, AG, SA, etc, will be as familiar to readers as are such English abbreviations as SN, Co, Corp, etc. After the name of a ship-owner, the location mentioned in each case is the ship's home port, which is not necessarily where the shipowner has his head office.
An alphabetical list of all shipowners with their complete styles is given on pages 207/209 of this volume.

**Builders** Like shipowners, builders are noted throughout by their accepted short-forms, and are listed alphabetically with their complete styles on pages 210/211 of this volume.

**Completion** Completion-date is the date of commencement of trials.

**Routes** Ports of call are omitted from the information concerning routes.

# Contents

# New Ships for 'Italia'

Motorship *Giulio Cesare*
'Italia' SAN, Genoa

Builders: CR dell'Adriatico,
Monfalcone
Yard no: 1756
27,078 GRT; 207.6 × 26.6 m /
681 × 87.2 ft; FIAT diesel; Twin
screw; 37,000 BHP; 21, max 23.31
kn; Passengers: 178 1st class, 288
cabin class, 714 tourist class;
Crew: 493.

**1950** May 18: Launched.
**1951** Sep: Completed.
Oct 27: Maiden voyage Genoa-
Buenos Aires.
**1956** Jun 29: First voyage Genoa-
New York.
**1960** Genoa-La Plata service
again.
**1973** Jan 14: Laid up at Naples.
May 11: Arrived at La Spezia to
be broken up by Terrestre
Marittima.

Motorship *Augustus*
'Italia' SAN, Genoa

Builders: CR dell'Adriatico,
Trieste
Yard no: 1757
27,090 GRT; 207.3 × 26.6 m /
680 × 87.2 ft; FIAT diesel; Twin
screw; 37,000 BHP; 21, max over
23 kn; Passengers: 178 1st class,
288 cabin class, 714 tourist class;
Crew: 493.

**1950** Nov 19: Launched.
**1952** Feb: Completed.
Mar: Maiden voyage Genoa-
Buenos Aires.
**1957** Feb 7: First voyage Genoa-
New York.
**1961** Genoa-La Plata service
again.
**1976** Jan 16: Laid up at Naples.

*1/2 The* Giulio Cesare *(2) was
launched in 1950, the first ship of an
extensive new construction programme
for Italian passenger shipping. She
entered the South American service
with her sister ship* Augustus *(1).*

1

Turbine steamer *Andrea Doria*
'Italia' SAN, Genoa

Builders: Ansaldo, Sestri Ponente
Yard no: 918
29,083 GRT; 213.4 × 27.5 m /
700 × 90.2 ft; Parsons geared
turbines, Stabilimento Mekaniko;
Twin screw; 50,000 SHP; 23, max
25.3 kn; Passengers: 218 1st class,
320 cabin class, 703 tourist class;
Crew: 563.

**1951** Jun 16: Launched.
**1952** Dec 9: Completed.
**1953** Jan 14: Maiden voyage
Genoa-New York.
**1956** Jul 25: *Andrea Doria* was
rammed by the Swedish America
liner *Stockholm* in thick fog 100
nautical miles from New York.
The ships had been in radar
contact and had made course and
speed ajustments but nevertheless
they collided. In the subsequent
enquiry it proved impossible to
reconstruct the sequence of events
with absolute certainty. The
responsible officers of both ships
were nevertheless reproached for
faulty navigation.
Shortly before midnight the bow
of the *Stockholm* drove with
considerable force into the
starboard side of the *Andrea
Doria* at the level of the bridge
and tore a gash 18 m (58 ft) wide
in the hull. The Italian ship
rapidly developed a heavy list, so
much so that the port boats could
no longer be lowered. An SOS call
was immediately made and work
started to get the passengers and a
part of the crew into those boats
which could be launched. The
*Stockholm*, which was badly
damaged but still afloat, took
533 people aboard from the

*Andrea Doria* before heading
back to New York with her
shattered forepart. Meanwhile
other ships had arrived on the
scene in response to the SOS call.
The *Ile de France* took 760 people
aboard, the US transport *Private
William H. Thomas* 156, the
United Fruit liner *Cape Ann* 129,
and the US destroyer *Edward H.
Allen* 76.
The *Andrea Doria* heeled over and
sank in the afternoon of July 26,
12 hours after the collision. The
disaster claimed 47 lives from the
Italian ship and five from the
*Stockholm*.

Turbine steamer *Cristoforo
Colombo*
'Italia' SAN, Genoa

Builders: Ansaldo, Sestri Ponene
Yard no: 1478
29,191 GRT; 213.4 × 27.5 m /
700 × 90.2 ft; Parsons geared
turbines from builders; Twin
screw; 50,000 SHP; 23, max over
25 kn; Passengers: 222 1st class,
222 cabin class, 640 tourist class;
Crew: 563.

**1953** May 10: Launched.
**1954** Jul: Completed.
Jul 15: Maiden voyage Genoa-
New York.
**1963** Jan-March: Passenger
accommodation refitted. 222 1st
class, 640 tourist class. 29,429
GRT.
**1965** Jun 3: First voyage Trieste-
New York.
**1973** Feb 1: Entered the Trieste-
Genoa-La Plata service *vice* the
*Giulio Cesare*, which had been
laid up.

**3** *The* Andrea Doria *sank in 1956 afte*
*a collision in fog with the Swedish line*
Stockholm.
**4** *Like her sister ship* Andrea Doria,
*the* Cristoforo Colombo *was used in*
*the New York service. From the mid-*
*'60s onwards the 'Italia' North*
*Atlantic liners had white hulls.*

Turbine steamer *Leonardo da Vinci*
'Italia' SAN, Genoa

Builders: Ansaldo, Sestri Ponente
Yard no: 1550
33,340 GRT; 233.9 × 28.1 m /
767 × 92.1 ft; Parsons geared
turbines from builders; Twin
screw; 52,000 SHP; 23, max 25.3
kn; Passengers: 413 1st class, 342
cabin class, 571 tourist class;
Crew: 580.

**1958** Dec 7: Launched.
**1960** May 19: Trials.
Jun 17: Sailed on first voyage, a
Mediterranean cruise.
Jun 30: Maiden voyage Genoa-
New York.
**1965** Jul 19: First voyage Naples-
New York.
Cruising.

**5** *The* Leonardo da Vinci *entered
service in 1960 as a replacement
for the* Andrea Doria.

5

Motorship *Australia*
Lloyd Triestino, Genoa

1963 *Donizetti*

Builders: CR dell'Adriatico,
Trieste
Yard no: 1758
12,839 GRT; 161.0 × 21.1 m /
528 × 69.2 ft; Sulzer diesels from
builders; Twin screw; 14,000
BHP; 18 kn; Passengers: 280 1st

class, 120 2nd class, 392 3rd class;
Crew: 236.

**1950** May 21: Launched.
**1951** Apr: Completed.
Apr 19: Maiden voyage Trieste-
Sydney, then Genoa-Sydney
service.
**1959** 13,140 GRT. Passengers:
136 1st class, 536 tourist class.
**1963** Apr 4: To 'Italia' SAN.
Jun: Renamed *Donizetti*.

Genoa-Central America-
Valparaiso service. 13,226 GRT.
**1976** Oct 15: Laid up at La
Spezia.

**1** *The* Australia *was the first of three
motorships in the Lloyd Triestino
Australia service.*

1

Motorship *Oceania*
Lloyd Triestino, Genoa

1963 *Verdi*

Builders: CR dell'Adriatico,
Trieste
Yard no: 1759
12,839 GRT; 160.6 × 21.1 m /
527 × 69.2 ft; Sulzer diesels from
builders; Twin screw; 14,000
BHP; 18 kn; Passengers: 280 1st
class, 120 2nd class, 392 3rd class;
Crew: 236.

**1950** Jul 30: Launched.
**1951** Aug: Completed.
Aug 18: Maiden voyage Genoa-
Sydney.
**1959** 13,139 GRT. Passengers:
136 1st class, 536 tourist class.
**1963** May 4: To 'Italia' SAN.
Jul: Renamed *Verdi*.
13,226 GRT. Genoa-Central
America-Valparaiso service.
**1976** Jul 27: Laid up at Genoa.

Motorship *Neptunia*
Lloyd Triestino, Genoa

1963 *Rossini*

Builders: CR dell'Adriatico,
Trieste
Yard no: 1760
12,838 GRT; 160.9 × 21.1 m /
528 × 69.2 ft; Sulzer diesels from
builders; Twin screw; 14,000 BHP;
18 kn; Passengers: 280 1st class,
120 2nd class, 392 3rd class; Crew:
236.

**1950** Oct 1: Launched.
**1951** Sep: Completed.
Sep 14: Maiden voyage Genoa-
Sydney.
**1959** 13,141 GRT. Passengers:
136 1st class, 536 tourist class.
**1963** Oct 20: To 'Italia' SAN.
Dec: Renamed *Rossini*.
13,225 GRT. Genoa-Central
America-Valparaiso service.
**1976** Aug 26: Laid up at Genoa.
Nov 19: Laid up at La Spezia.

*2/3 The* Oceania *was sold to 'Italia' in
1963, as were her sister ships. (3)
shows the ship as the* Verdi *in the
Panama Canal.*
*4 The motorship* Neptunia.

2

Motorship *Africa*
Lloyd Triestino, Trieste

1976 *Protea*

Builders: CR dell'Adriatico,
Monfalcone
Yard no: 1763
11,427 GRT; 159.3 × 20.8 m /
523 × 68.2 ft; Sulzer diesels from
builders; Twin screw; 16,100
BHP; 19.5, max 21.5 kn;
Passengers: 148 1st class, 252
cabin class, 84 tourist class; Crew:
215.

**1951** Jan 24: Launched.
**1952** Feb: Completion and
maiden voyage Genoa-Cape
Town.
**1953** Genoa-Cape Town.
**1960** Passenger accommodation:
148 1st class, 298 tourist class.
11,434 GRT.
**1967** Trieste-Cape Town-
Mombasa.
**1976** Jan 31: Laid up at Trieste.
Dec: Renamed *Protea*.

Motorship *Europa*
Lloyd Triestino, Trieste

1976 *Blue Sea*

Builders: Ansaldo, La Spezia
Yard no: 319
11,430 GRT; 158.0 × 20.8 m /
518 × 68.2 ft; FIAT diesels from
builders; Twin screw; 16,100
BHP; 19.5, max 21.5 kn;
Passengers: 148 1st class, 252
cabin class; 84 tourist class; Crew:
213.

**1951** Oct 21: Launched.
**1952** Oct: Completion and
maiden voyage Trieste-Cape
Town.
**1953** Genoa-Cape Town.
**1960** Passengers: 148 1st class,
298 tourist class. 11,440 GRT.
**1967** Trieste-Cape Town-
Mombasa.
**1976** Sep: Sold to Ahmed
Mohamed Baaboud, Jeddah.
Renamed *Blue Sea*.
Nov 12: Fire broke out while at
Jeddah. Passengers safely
disembarked. Ship sank at her
anchorage during night of
November 14/15.

*5/6 During the period 1951 to 1953
Lloyd Triestino had four ships built of
the same type.* Africa *and* Europa *were
for the South Africa service.*

Motorship *Victoria*
Lloyd Triestino, Trieste

Builders: CR dell'Adriatico, San
Marco
Yard no: 1765
11,695 GRT; 158.4 × 20.7 m /
520 × 67.9 ft; FIAT diesels from
builders; 16,100 BHP; 19.5, max
21.6 kn; Twin screw; Passengers:
286 1st class, 181 tourist class;
Crew: 213.

**1951** Sep 18: Launched.
**1953** Mar: Completion and
maiden voyage Venice-Far East.
Then Genoa-Hong Kong service.
**1965** Trieste-Hong Kong.
**1967** Trieste-Hong Kong-
Karachi.
**1974** Oct: Sold to 'Adriatica'
SAN, Venice. Trieste-Beirut
service and cruising.

Motorship *Asia*
Lloyd Triestino, Trieste

1975 *Persia*

Builders: CR dell'Adriatico, San
Marco
Yard no: 1766
11,693 GRT; 158.4 × 20.7 m /
520 × 67.9 ft; FIAT diesels from
builders; Twin screw; 16,100
BHP; 19.5, max 21.5 kn;
Passengers: 286 1st class, 181
tourist class; Crew: 213.

**1951** Oct 28: Launched.
**1953** Apr: Completion and
maiden voyage Venice-Hong
Kong. Then Genoa-Hong Kong
service.
**1965** Trieste-Hong Kong.
**1967** Trieste-Cape Town-
Karachi.
**1975** Apr 11: Laid up at Trieste.
Jun 30: Sold to Rashid Fares
Enterprises, Beirut. Renamed
*Persia*. Rebuilt as a livestock
transport.

**7/8** Victoria *and* Asia *were used in the*
*Genoa-Hong Kong service.*

Turbine steamer *Independence*
American Export Lines, New
York

1974 *Oceanic Independence*
1976 *Sea Luck 1*

Builders: Bethlehem Steel Co,
Quincy
Yard no: 1618
23,719 GRT; 208.0 × 27.2 m /
682 × 89.2 ft; Geared turbines
from builders; Twin screw; 55,000
SHP; 23, max 26.15 kn;
Passengers: 295 1st class, 375
cabin class, 330 tourist class.

**1950** Jun 3: Launched.
**1951** Jan: Completed.
Feb 11: Maiden voyage (cruise)
New York-Mediterranean.
Apr 12: New York-Genoa, later
New York-Naples service.
**1959** Feb-Apr: Passenger
accommodation refitted at
Newport News. 110 more 1st class
passengers. 23,754 GRT.
**1967** 20,251 GRT.
**1968** The American travel agency

Fugazi started using the
*Independence* as a 'funship' for a
new style of cruising. She was
refitted as a one-class vessel, and
her interior and exterior given
pop-art decoration.
**1969** Mar 13: Laid up at
Baltimore.
**1974** Jan: Sold to Atlantic Far
East Lines Inc, Monrovia
(C.Y. Tung).
Renamed *Oceanic Independence*.
950 passengers in one class.
Cruising.
**1976** Jan 19: Laid up at Hong
Kong.
Nov: Renamed *Sea Luck 1*.
Registered at Panama.


Turbine steamer *Constitution*
American Export Lines, New
York

1974 *Oceanic Constitution*

Builders: Bethlehem Steel Co,
Quincy

Yard no: 1619
23,754 GRT; 207.8 × 27.2 m /
682 × 89.2 ft; Geared turbines
from builders; Twin screw; 55,000
SHP; 23, max over 26 kn;
Passengers: 295 1st class, 375
cabin class, 330 tourist class.

**1950** Sep 16: Launched.
**1951** Jun: Completed.
Jun 25: Maiden voyage New York-
Naples-Genoa.
**1959** Jan-Mar: 1st class passenger
accommodation refitted at
**Newport News. 484 1st class**
passengers. 23,754 GRT.
**1967** 20,269 GRT.
**1968** Cruising only.
Sep 9: Laid up at Jacksonville.
**1974** Jan: Sold to Atlantic Far
East Lines Inc, Monrovia
(C.Y. Tung).
Renamed *Oceanic Constitution*.
950 passengers in one class.
**1974** Aug 4: Laid up at Hong
Kong.

1

**1/2** *Built for the New York-Mediter-ranean service, the sister ships* Independence (*1*) *and* Constitution (*2*) *were refitted in 1959. See bridge front and promenade deck in* (*2*).

**3** *In 1968 the American travel agency Fugazi painted the* Independence *in these colours for cruising.*

Turbine steamer *Oronsay*
Orient Line, London

Builders: Vickers-Armstrongs,
Barrow
Yard no: 976
27,632 GRT; 216.0 × 28.5 m /
708 × 93.5 ft; Parsons geared
turbines from builders; Twin
screw; 42,500 SHP; 22, max
25.8 m /84.6 ft; Passengers: 668
1st class, 833 tourist class; Crew:
622.

**1950** Jun 30: Launched.
**1951** May: Completed.
May 16: Maiden voyage
London-Sydney.
**1954** Jan 1: The service was
extended beyond Sydney to Los
Angeles.
**1960** May: The *Oronsay* was
integrated into P & O-Orient
Lines.
**1966** Owners became P & O after
the last Orient shares had been
acquired by the latter.
**1969** 28,117 GRT.
**1970** 28,136 GRT.
**1975** Oct 7: Arrived at Kaohsiung
to be broken up by Nan Feng
Steel Enterprise Co.

Turbine steamer *Orsova*
Orient Line, London

Builders: Vickers-Armstrongs,
Barrow
Yard no: 1021
28,790 GRT; 220.3 × 27.5 m /
723 × 90.2 ft; Parsons geared
turbines from builders; Twin
screw; 42,500 SHP; 22, max 26
kn; Passengers: 681 1st class, 813
tourist class; Crew: 620.

**1953** May 14: Launched.
**1954** Mar: Completed.
Mar 17: Maiden voyage London-
Sydney.
**1955** Apr 27: London-Sydney-
San Francisco-London service.
**1960** May: Owners became
P & O-Orient Lines.
**1966** Owners became P & O Line,
as *Oronsay*.
**1969** 29,091 GRT.
**1974** Feb 14: Arrived at
Kaohsiung to be broken up.

*1/2 The* Oronsay *(1) in P & O colours
in 1966, and her near-sister ship*
Orsova *in the old Orient Line colours.*

Turbine steamer *Arcadia*
P & O Line, London

Builders: Brown, Clydebank
Yard no: 675
29,734 GRT; 219.7 × 27.5 m /
721 × 90.2 ft; geared turbines
from builders; Twin screw; 42,500
SHP; 22, max over 25 kn;
Passengers: 675 1st class, 735
tourist class; Crew: 710.

**1953**  May 14: Launched.
**1954**  Feb: Completed.
Feb 22: Maiden voyage London-
Sydney.
**1959**  Oct 19: First voyage London-
Sydney-Transpacific-London.
Cruising.
**1960**  29,664 GRT.
**1967**  29,871 GRT.

Turbine steamer *Iberia*
P & O Line, London

Builders: Harland & Wolff,
Belfast
Yard no: 1476
29,614 GRT; 219.0 × 27.5 m /
718 × 90.2 ft; Geared turbines,
H & W; Twin screw; 42,500 SHP;
22, max over 25 kn; Passengers:
673 1st class, 733 tourist class;
Crew: 711.

**1954**  Jan 21: Launched.
**1954**  Sep: Completed.
Sep 28: Maiden voyage London-
Sydney.
**1959**  Dec 16: First voyage
London-Sydney-San Francisco-
London. Cruising.
**1970**  29,779 GRT.
**1972**  Apr 19: Laid up at
Southampton.
Sep 5: Arrived at Kaohsiung.
Broken up by Tung Cheng Steel
Corp.

**3/4** *The P & O liners* Iberia *and*
Arcadia (*4*) *which entered service in*
*1954.*

3

4

# Three New British Ships

Turbine steamer *Ocean Monarch*
Furness, Withy & Co, London

1967 *Varna*

Builders: Vickers-Armstrongs,
Newcastle
Yard no: 119
13,654 GRT; 157.3 × 22.0 m /
516 × 72.2 ft; Parsons geared
turbines from builders; Twin
screw; 11,500 SHP; 18 kn;
Passengers: 414 1st class.

**1950** Jul 27: Launched.
**1951** Mar 23: Commencement of
trials.
Apr 18: Maiden voyage London-
New York.
May 3: First voyage New York-
Bermuda.
**1961** 13,581 GRT.
**1966** Sep 22: Laid up on River
Fal.
**1967** Aug: Sold to the Bulgarian
shipping company Balkanturist at
Varna. Renamed *Varna*. Used for
cruising.

Motorship *Ruahine*
New Zealand Line, London

1968 *Oriental Rio*

Builders: Brown, Clydebank
Yard no: 658
17,851 GRT; 178.2 × 22.9 m /
584 × 75,1 ft; Doxford diesels,
Brown; Twin screw; 14,200 BHP;
17 kn; Passengers: 267 in one
class.

**1950** Dec 11: Launched.
**1951** May: Completed.
May 22: Maiden voyage London-
Wellington.
**1966** Jan: New Zealand Line
adopted the funnel colours of the
Federal SN Co. Both companies
belonged to the P & O group.
**1968** The *Ruahine* was bought by
C.Y.Tung and registered as the
*Oriental Rio* for the Chinese
Maritime Trust Ltd, Taipeh.
**1969** Feb: First voyage in
round-the-world-service.
**1970** 17,730 GRT, later 17,789

GRT.
**1973** Dec 31: Arrived at
Kaohsiung to be broken up.

1 *The Bulgarian* Varna *was launched
in 1950 as the* Ocean Monarch *for
Furness, Withy & Co.*
2/3 *The* Ruahine (2), *which was used
in the London-Wellington service, wa
renamed* Oriental Rio *in 1968.*

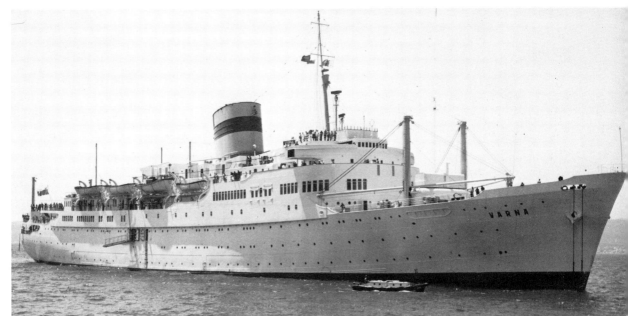

1

2

3

Motorship *Aureol*
Elder Dempster Lines, Liverpool

1975 *Marianna VI*

Builders: Stephen, Glasgow
Yard no: 629
14,083 GRT; 163.6 × 21.4 m /
537 × 70.2 ft; Doxford diesels
from builders; Twin screw; 10,800
SHP; 16 kn; Passengers: 253 1st
class, 100 cabin class; Crew: 145.

**1951** Mar 28: Launched.
Oct: Completed.
Nov 3: Maiden voyage Liverpool-
Lagos.
**1972** Apr 26: First voyage
Southampton-Lagos.
**1974** Oct 18: Arrived for last time
at Southampton. Sold to
Marianna Shipping & Trading
Co, Panama.
Nov: Arrived at Piraeus for refit.
**1975** Jan: Renamed *Marianna
VI*.
Mar 21: Laid up at Jeddah.

**4** *The Elder Dempster liner* Aureol *in Hamburg harbour.*

4

Turbine steamer *Provence*
SGTM, Marseille

1965 *Enrico C.*

Builders: Swan, Hunter &
Wigham Richardson, Newcastle
Yard no: 1874
15,889 GRT; 176.7 × 22.3 m /
580 × 73.1 ft; Parsons geared
turbines; Twin screw; 15,000
SHP; 18, max 20 kn; Passengers:
157 1st class, 167 tourist class,
508 3rd class in cabins, 470 3rd
class in dormitories.

**1950** Aug 15: Launched.
**1951** Mar: Completed.
Mar 30: Maiden voyage Marseille-
Buenos Aires.
**1954** Feb 18: The *Provence*
collided with the Liberian tanker
*Saxonsea* on the La Plata, and
was so badly damaged that she
did not arrive back at Marseille
until January 1 1955, after
provisional repairs at Buenos
Aires. The damage was finally
repaired at Marseille.
**1955** Mar 26: First voyage after
the accident.
**1962** First voyage Genoa-Buenos
Aires under charter to Costa
Armatori, Genoa.
**1965** Sold to Costa Armatori,
Genoa. Renamed *Enrico C.*
Refitted at Genoa. Passengers:
218 1st class, 980 tourist class.
13,607 GRT.
**1966** First voyage Genoa-Buenos
Aires.
**1972** Cruising only.

*1/2 Built for the South America
service, the* Provence *(1) was sold to
Italy in 1965 to become the* Encrico C.
*(2).*

1

Turbine steamer *Bretagne*
SGTM Marseille

1962 *Brittany*

Builders: Penhoët, St Nazaire
Yard no: X12
16,335 GRT; 177.0 × 22.3 m /
581 × 73.1 ft; Parsons geared
turbines from builders; Twin
screw; 15,000 SHP; 18, max 20
kn; Passengers: 149 1st class, 167
tourist class, 606 3rd class in
cabins, 368 3rd class in
dormitories.

**1951** Jul 20: Launched.
**1952** Jan: Completed.
Feb 14: Maiden voyage Marseille-
Buenos Aires. She had previously
made two short cruises.
**1960** Nov 18: Chartered to D. &
A. Chandris. Passenger
accommodation refitted at Genoa.
150 1st class, 1,050 tourist class.
**1961** May 3: First voyage Piraeus-
Sydney followed by some cruising
from New York.
Sep 20: Chandris bought the
*Bretagne* which was registered at
Piraeus for the Europe-Australia
Line.
Sep 22: First voyage
Southampton-Brisbane, then
Southampton-Sydney service.
**1962** Renamed *Brittany*.
**1963** Mar 28: The *Brittany* went
to Skaramanga for engine repairs
at the Hellenic Shipyards. She
caught fire there on April 8 and
was completely destroyed. The
burning wreck was beached in
Vasilika Bay on the night of
April 9.
May 10: Raised and laid up.
**1964** Mar 31: Arrived at La
Spezia, and there broken up by
Cantieri Santa Maria.

**3** *The* Bretagne, *sister ship of the*
Provence, *shown here after her sale to*
Chandris.

2

3

# The Yapeyú Class

Motorship *Yapeyú*
Cia Argentina de Nav Dodero,
Buenos Aires

1969 *Petrel*
1974 *Cremona*
1976 *Iran Cremona*

Builders: Van der Giessen,
Krimpen
Yard no: 753
11,450 GRT; 158.6 × 19.6 m /
520 × 64.3 ft; Sulzer diesels,
Werkspoor; Twin screw; 12,000
BHP; 18 kn; Passengers: 13 1st
class, 740 tourist class; Crew: 165.

**1950** Oct 17: Launched.
**1951** Apr: Completed. Buenos
Aires-Hamburg service.
**1955** Owners' name changed to
FANU.
**1962** FANU and Flota Mercante
del Estado combined to form
ELMA.
**1964** First voyage in Buenos
Aires-Genoa service.
**1969** Sold to Transportes
Oceanicos SA, Buenos Aires.
Renamed *Petrel*.
**1971** Entered service as livestock
transport between Australia and
the Persian Gulf.
**1973** Sold to Transagro SA
Naviera y Agropecuria, Buenos
Aires.
**1974** Oct: Resold to Cormoran SS
Co, Singapore. Renamed
*Cremona*.
**1976** Renamed *Iran Cremona*.

Motorship *Maipu*
Cia Argentina de Nav Dodero,
Buenos Aires

Builders: 'De Schelde', Vlissingen
Yard no: 267
11,515 GRT; 158.6 × 19.6 m /
520 × 64.3 ft; Sulzer diesels from
builders; Twin screw; 12,000
BHP; 18 kn; Passengers: 13 1st
class, 740 tourist class; Crew: 165.

**1951** Jan 20: Launched.
May: Completed.
Buenos Aires-Hamburg service.
Nov 4: Bound for Hamburg in
thick fog the *Maipu* was in
collision with the transport
*General M.L. Hersey*, which had
3,000 troops on board, northwest
of the Weser lightship. The badly
damaged *Maipu* began to sink.
The 107 passengers and the crew
were picked up before the ship
went down three hours after the
collision.

Motorship *Alberto Dodero*
Cia Argentina de Nav Dodero,
Buenos Aires

1969 *Cormoran*

Builders: 'De Schelde', Vlissingen
Yard no: 268
11,521 GRT; 158.6 × 19.6 m /
520 × 64.3 ft; Sulzer diesels from
builders; Twin screw; 12,000
BHP; 18 kn; Passengers: 13 1st
class, 740 tourist class; Crew: 165.

**1951** Jun 30: Launched.
**1951** Oct: Completed.
Buenos Aires-Hamburg service.
**1955** Owners' name changed to
FANU.
**1962** May 24: FANU combined
with Flota Mercante del Estado to
form ELMA.
**1964** First voyage in Buenos
Aires-Genoa service.
**1969** Sold to Transportes
Oceanicos SA, Buenos Aires.
Renamed *Cormoran*.
**1971** First voyage as livestock
transport between Fremantle and
the Persian Gulf.
**1973** Sold to Transagro SA
Naviera y Agropecuria, Buenos
Aires.
**1974** Sold to Cormoran SS Co,
Singapore.

**1** *The motorship* Yapeyú *with the
FANU funnel markings and white
hull.*
**2** *The* Maipu, *which sank in 1951 after
a collision, in Dodero Line colours.*
**3** *A photograph of the* Alberto Dodero
*in 1963.*

1

2

3

## Kenya and Uganda

Turbine steamer *Kenya*
British India Line, London

Builders: Barclay, Curle & Co,
Glasgow
Yard no: 719
14,464 GRT; 164.5 × 21.7 m /
540 × 71.2 ft; Parsons geared
turbines; Twin screw; 12,300
SHP; 16, max 19.16 kn;
Passengers: 194 1st class, 103
tourist class.

**1950** Nov 28: Launched.
**1951** Aug: Completed.
Aug 22: Maiden voyage London-
Beira.
**1969** Jul 2: Arrived at La Spezia.
Broken up by Cantieri di
Portovenere.

Turbine steamer *Uganda*
British India Line, London

Builders: Barclay, Curle & Co,
Glasgow
Yard no: 720
14,430 GRT; 164.4 × 21.7 m /
539 × 71.2 ft; Geared turbines,
Wallsend slipway; Twin screw;
12,300 SHP; 16, max 19.25 kn;
Passengers: 167 1st class, 133
tourist class.

**1952** Jan 15: Launched.
Jul 17: Completed.
Aug 2: Maiden voyage London-
Beira.
**1967** Apr 5: Arrived at
Howaldtswerke Hamburg, where
she was rebuilt as a scholars'
cruise-liner.

**1968** Feb 15: In service after
completion of rebuilding. 16,907
GRT. Accommodation for 1,224
schoolchildren.
Feb 27: First scholars' cruise.
**1973** The ships of British India
Line, which belonged to the
P & O group, were registered
under the ownership of P & O
Line.

1/2 *The British India liner* Kenya, *(1)
with a black hull during her early pre-
1955 service years.*
3 *Sister ship to the* Kenya, *the* Uganda
*was extensively rebuilt for scholars'
cruises in 1967/68 (3).*

1

2

3

# Ryndam and Maasdam

Turbine steamer *Ryndam*
Holland-America Line,
Rotterdam

1968 *Waterman*
1968 *Ryndam*
1972 *Atlas*

Builders: Wilton-Fijenoord,
Schiedam
Yard no: 732
15,015 GRT; 153.2 × 21.1 m /
502 × 69.2 ft; Geared turbines,
General Electric Co; Single screw;
8,500 SHP; 16.5 kn; Passengers:
39 1st class, 854 tourist class;
Crew: 300.

**1949** Laid down as passenger-
cargo vessel *Dinteldyk*.
**1950** Dec 19: Launched as
*Ryndam*.
**1951** Jul: Completed.
Jul 16: Maiden voyage Rotterdam-
New York.

**1966** Sep 14: Handed over to
Europe-Canada Line, Bremen.
Bremerhaven-New York service.
15,051 GRT.
**1968** May 24: Transferred to NV
Mij Transoceaan, a subsidiary of
Holland-America Line. Renamed
*Waterman*.
Oct 10: Back to Holland-America
Line. Renamed *Ryndam*. North
Atlantic service and cruising.
**1971** Jun: Laid up at Schiedam.
**1972** Aug 18: To World Wide
Cruises SA, Panama. Renamed
*Atlas*. Rebuilt at Piraeus as a
cruise liner. 9,114 GRT.
**1973** May 5: First Mediterranean
cruise for Epirotiki Line.

**1-3** *The Holland-America liner*
Ryndam, *shown under the German
flag (2), has been cruising in the
Mediterranean as the* Atlas *(3) since
1972.*

1

## 3

Turbine steamer *Maasdam*
Holland-America Line,
Rotterdam

1968 *Stefan Batory*

Builders: Wilton-Fijenoord,
Schiedam
Yard no: 733
15,024 GRT; 153.2 × 21.1 m /
502 × 69.2 ft; Geared turbines,
General Electric Co; Single screw;
8,500 SHP; 16.5 kn; Passengers:
39 1st class, 842 tourist class;
Crew: 300.

**1949** Planned as passenger-cargo
vessel *Diemerdyk*.
**1952** Apr 5: Launched.
Jul 15: Completed.
Aug 11: Maiden voyage
Rotterdam-New York.
**1963** Feb 15: On her first visit to
Bremerhaven whither the New
York service had been extended,
the *Maasdam* struck the sunken
wrecks in the mouth of the Weser
of the British *Harborough* and the
Soviet *Kholmogory*. This occurred
because navigational buoys had
been moved out of position by
drifting ice. The *Maasdam*
received heavy underwater
damage and her master gave the
order for the 500 passengers to
take to the boats. The ship was
later taken to the North German
Lloyd repair yard.
Apr 16: First voyage
Bremerhaven-New York.
**1966** Rotterdam-Montreal
service.
**1968** Sold to Polish Ocean Lines,
Gdynia. Renamed *Stefan Batory*.
Refitted at Gdynia.
**1969** Apr 11: First voyage
Gdynia-Montreal.

**4/5** *In 1968 the* Maasdam *(4) went to
Poland as the* Stefan Batory *(5).*

**Tanker and Passenger Vessel San Lorenzo**

Motorship *San Lorenzo*
Yacimientos Petroliferos Fiscales,
Buenos Aires

Builders: P. Smit jr, Rotterdam
Yard no: 598
11,674 GRT; 170.1 × 20.7 m /
558 × 67.9 ft; Burmeister &
Wain diesels from builders; Single
screw; 9,300 BHP; 16 kn;
Passengers: 20 1st class, 40 3rd
class; Crew: 83.

**1950** Oct 21: Launched.
**1951** Mar 6: Trials.
Entered Buenos Aires-Comodoro
Rivadavia service.

**1** *The tanker and packet vessel* San
Lorenzo *had accommodation for 60
passengers.*

1

Motorship *Monte Ulia*
Naviera Aznar, Bilbao

Launched as *Monasterio de el Escorial*
1976 *Climax Opal*

Builders: Soc Española de Construccion Naval, Bilbao
Yard no: 66
10,123 GRT; 148.5 × 19.0 m / 487 × 62.3 ft; Sulzer diesels;
Single screw; 7,300 BHP; 16.5 kn;
Passengers: 64 1st class, 146 2nd class.

**1951** Jan 9: Launched as *Monasterio de el Escorial* for the Spanish state shipping company Empresa Nacional Elcano SA.
**1952** Sold to Naviera Aznar. Renamed *Monte Ulia*.

Mar: Completed.
Genoa-Vera Cruz service.
**1962** London-Teneriffe service, and Cadiz-Teneriffe in the summer months.
**1974** Liverpool-Teneriffe service.
**1976** Jul: Sold to Climax Shipping Corp, Monrovia. Singapore flag. Renamed *Climax Opal*.

**1** *The* Monte Ulia *entered the Genoa-Central America service in 1952.*

1

Motorship *Guadalupe*
Cia Trasatlantica, Barcelona

Launched as *Monasterio de Guadalupe*

Builders: Soc Española de Construccion Naval, Bilbao
Yard no: 67
10,226 GRT; 148.5 × 19.0 m / 487 × 62.3 ft; Sulzer diesels from builders; Single screw; 7,300 BHP; 16.5 kn; Passengers: 105 1st class, 244 tourist class.

**1951** May 2: Launched as *Monasterio de Guadalupe* for Empresa Nacional Elcano SA.
**1952** Sold to Cia Trasatlantica. Renamed *Guadalupe*.
**1953** Mar: Completed.
Mar 21: Maiden voyage Bilbao-New York-Vera Cruz.
**1973** Apr 10: Arrived at Castellon to be broken up.

Motorship *Covadonga*
Cia Trasatlántica, Barcelona

Launched as *Monasterio de la Rabida*

Builders: Soc Euskalduna, Bilbao
Yard no: 134
10,226 GRT; 148.5 × 19.0 m / 487 × 62.3 ft; Sulzer diesels from builders; Single screw; 7,300 BHP; 16.5 kn; Passengers: 105 1st class, 248 tourist class.

**1951** Oct 31: Launched as *Monasterio de la Rabida* for Empress Nacional Elcano SA.
**1952** To Cia Trasatlantica. Renamed *Covadonga*.
**1953** May: Completed.
May: The *Covadonga* made her maiden voyage to London for the coronation of Queen Elizabeth II.
Aug 27: First voyage Bilbao-New York-Vera Cruz.
**1973** Apr 4: Arrived at Castellon to be broken up.

*2-4 The* Guadelupe *(2) and (3) and* Covadonga *served on the North Atlantic route for Cia Trasatlantica.*

2

Turbine steamer *Rhodesia Castle*
Union-Castle Line, London

Builders: Harland & Wolff,
Belfast
Yard no: 1431
17,041 GRT; 175.5 × 22.6 m /
576 × 74.1 ft; Geared turbines,
H & W; Twin screw; 14,400 SHP;
17.5 kn; Passengers: 526 cabin
class.

**1951** Apr 5: Launched.
Nov: Completed.

London-round Africa service.
**1967** May 4: Laid up in
Blackwater River.
Oct 26: Arrived at Kaohsiung.
Broken up by Chin Ho Fa Steel &
Iron Co.

1

**1/2** *The* Rhodesia Castle *before (1) and after (2) the heightening of her funnel in 1961.*

Turbine steamer *Kenya Castle*
Union-Castle Line, London

1967 *Amerikanis*

Builders: Harland & Wolff,
Belfast
Yard no: 1432
17,041 GRT; 175.5 × 22.6 m /
576 × 74.1 ft; Geared turbines,
H & W; Twin screw; 14,400 SHP;
17.5 kn; Passengers: 526 cabin
class.

**1951** Jun 21: Launched.
**1952** Feb: Completed.
Apr 4: Maiden voyage London-
round Africa.
**1967** Apr 22: Laid up on River
Blackwater.
Aug: Sold to the Chandris group
and registered under the
ownership of the National
Hellenic American Line SA at
Piraeus. Renamed *Amerikanis*.

Refitted at Piraeus for North
Atlantic service and cruising.
19,904 GRT.
**1968** Aug 8: First voyage
Piraeus-New York. Since then,
cruising from New York.
**1970** 16,485 GRT.

Turbine steamer *Braemer Castle*
Union-Castle Line, London

Builders: Harland & Wolff,
Belfast
Yard no: 1459
17,029 GRT; 175.5 × 22.6 m /
576 × 74.1 ft; Geared turbines,
H & W; Twin screw; 14,400 SHP;
17.5 kn; Passengers: 552 cabin
class.

**1952** Apr 24: Launched.
Nov: Completed.
Nov 22: Maiden voyage London-
round Africa.
**1965** Cruising only.
**1966** Jan 6: Arrived at Faslane to
be broken up by Shipbreaking
Industries.

3

**3-5** *The* Kenya Castle *(3) and* Braemar Castle *(5), respectively the second and third ships of the class, came into service in 1952. (4) shows the* Amerikanis *ex* Kenya Castle.

**Antilles and Flandre**

Turbine steamer *Antilles*
CGT, Le Havre

Builders: Arsenal de Brest
19,828 GRT; 182.8 × 24.5 m /
600 × 80.4 ft; Rateau geared
turbines, Ch de Bretagne; Twin
screw; 44,000 SHP; 22 kn;
Passengers: 404 1st class, 285
cabin class, 89 tourist class; Crew:
360.

**1951** Apr 26: Launched.
**1953** Jan 3: Delivered.
Following a cruise to Portugal and
North Africa and another in the
Mediterranean, in May 1953 the
*Antilles* made her maiden voyage
in the Le Havre-Central America
service.
**1971** Jan 8: During a voyage from
San Juan to Le Havre the *Antilles*
struck an unmarked underwater
reef off the Caribbean island of
Mustique. Escaping fuel caught
fire inside the ship, and the
situation quickly became so
critical that the 635 people on
board had to take to the boats.
They were picked up by the *Queen
Elizabeth 2*, the CGT ships

*Suffren* and *Point Allegre* as well
as by a number of smaller vessels
from Mustique. The *Antilles*
capsized the next day, still on fire.
On January 18 she broke in two.

Turbine steamer *Flandre*
CGT Le Havre

1968 *Carla C.*

Builders: A et Ch de France,
Dunkirk
Yard no: 206
20,469 GRT; 182.8 × 24.4 m /
600 × 80.0 ft; Rateau geared
turbines, Ch de Bretagne; Twin
screw; 44,000 SHP; 22 kn;
Passengers: 402 1st class, 285
cabin class, 97 tourist class; Crew:
361.

**1951** Oct 31: Launched.
**1952** Jul 8: Delivered.
Jul 23: Maiden voyage Le
Havre-New York. Because of
mechanical and electrical
troubles, she was withdrawn until
April 1953.
**1953** Apr 17: Le Havre-New York

service again.
**1955** Passenger accommodation:
212 1st class, 511 tourist class.
**1958** The *Flandre*, which had
hitherto sailed to Central America
in the winter with the *Antilles*,
was now placed on the New York
service all the year round.
**1962** Following the entry into
service of the *France*, the *Flandre*
was used only on the West Indies
service and for cruising. White
hull.
**1968** Feb: Sold to Costa
Armatori, Genoa. Renamed *Carla
C.* Refit commenced in Italy
which lasted until December.
19,975 GRT. 754 passengers.
**1969** Jan 10: First cruise Los
Angeles-Mexico. Since 1970,
cruising from US East Coast
ports.
**1974** Jun 1: The *Carla C.* arrived
at Amsterdam, where diesel
engines were substituted for her
geared turbines.
**1975** Jan: Back in service.

1

2

3

1 *The* Antilles, *built for CGT's Mediterranean service.*

2/3 *The* Flandre *sailed mainly on the Le Havre-New York route before changing in 1962 to the West Indies service and cruising, when her hull was painted white.* (3) *shows the* Carla C. *ex* Flandre.

# Vera Cruz and Santa Maria

Turbine steamer *Vera Cruz*
Cia Colonial, Lisbon

Builders: Cockerill, Hoboken
Yard no: 748
21,765 GRT; 185.9 × 23.1 m /
610 × 75.8 ft; Parsons geared
turbines from builders; 22,500
SHP; 20 kn; Passengers: 150 1st
class, 250 2nd class, 232 3rd class,
664 3rd in dormitories; Crew: 319.

**1951** Jun 2: Launched.
**1952** Feb: Completed. Lisbon-
Santos service. From 1953,
Lisbon-Buenos Aires. Also
alternated until 1956 with the
*Santa Maria* in the Central
America service.
**1960** The *Vera Cruz* was put on
the Lisbon-Angola route. After the
outbreak of trouble in Angola in
1961 she was used increasingly as a
troop transport.
**1973** Apr 19: Arrived at
Kaohsiung to be broken up.

Turbine steamer *Santa Maria*
Cia Colonial, Lisbon

Builders: Cockerill, Hoboken
Yard no: 749
20,906 GRT; 185.9 × 23.1 m /
610 × 75.8 ft; Parsons geared
turbines from builders; 22,500
SHP; 20 kn; Passengers: 150 1st
class, 250 2nd class, 232 3rd class,
660 3rd class in dormitories; Crew:
320.

**1952** Sep 20: Launched.
**1953** Sep: Completed. Lisbon-
Buenos Aires service. Also
alternated until 1956 with the *Vera
Cruz* in the Central America
service. Then solely
Lisbon-Central America,
including a call at Port
Everglades.
**1961** Jan 22: During a voyage
from Curaçao to Miami the *Santa
Maria* had reached the vicinity of
Martinique when a group of
armed rebels, who had come on
board as passengers at Curaçao,
overpowered the officers and took
over the liner. In the course of this
operation, the *Santa Maria's* third
officer was shot and several crew-
members wounded. The rebels,
opponents of the Portuguese head
of state Salazar, set course for
Angola, pursued by warships and
aircraft. The ship was sighted for
the first time on January 25. After
protracted radio negotiations the
leader of the rebels agreed to sail
to Brazil and release the 600
passengers. On January 28 the
*Santa Maria* changed course for
Brazil and arrived at Recife on
February 2, where the passengers
were allowed to disembark. The
rebels' plans to set sail again were
thwarted by a sit-down strike on

the part of the crew and by the
announcement that Portuguese
and Spanish warships were waiting
off Recife. They then surrendered.
**1973** Jul 19: Arrived at Kaohsiung
to be broken up.

*1/2 The Portuguese Central America
liners* Vera Cruz *(1) and* Santa Maria.
*The latter made the headlines in the
world's press for ten days in 1961 when
she was hijacked.*

**The United States**

Turbine steamer *United States*
United States Lines, New York

Builders: Newport News SB & DD Co
Yard no: 488
53,329 GRT; 301.8 × 31.0 m / 990 × 101.7 ft; Westinghouse geared turbines; Quadruple screw; 240,000 SHP; 31, max 40 kn; Passengers: 871 1st class, 508 cabin class, 549 tourist class; Crew: 1,093.

**1951** Jun 23: Floated in building dock.
**1952** Jun 21: Delivered.
Jul 3: Maiden voyage New York-Southampton. The *United States* broke all North Atlantic speed records. She sailed from the Ambrose lightship to Bishop Rock in three days, ten hours and 40 minutes at an average speed of 35.39 knots. On the homeward voyage she covered the same stretch in three days, 12 hours and 12 minutes at an average of 34.51 knots. This record has yet to be broken.
During the winter months her service was extended to Bremerhaven.
**1961** 51,988 GRT.
**1962** US measurement 44,893 GRT. Reduced to 38,216 GRT in 1967.
**1969** Nov 8: Laid up at Newport News; later at Hampton roads.
**1973** Feb: The US Maritime Administration bought the ship.
Laid up again at Norfolk, Va. Has since been offered for sale several times, always with the stipulation that she remain under the US flag.

**1** *The* United States, *the fastest commercial ship ever built.*

1

Motorship *La Bourdonnais*
Messageries Maritimes, Marseille

968 *Knossos*

Builders: Arsenal de Lorient
Yard no: MD2
10,944 GRT; 150.0 × 19.6 m /
492 × 64.3 ft; Burmeister & Wain
diesels, Penhoët; Twin screw;
12,500 BHP; 17, max 18.5 kn;
Passengers: 88 1st class, 112
tourist class, 299 3rd class.

1951 Jul 5: Launched.
1953 Feb: Completed.
Mar 31: Maiden voyage Marseille-
Mauritius.
1955 10,886 GRT.
1968 Sold to C.S. Efthymiadis,
Piraeus. Renamed *Knossos*.
Mediterranean service.

1973 May 3: During a voyage
from Piraeus to Limassol 186
passengers and 26 crew members
had to take to the boats when fire
broke out in the engine room. The
ship was towed back to Piraeus.
1976 Sold to Spanish
shipbreakers.

1 La Bourdonnais, *prototype of a
group of four vessels for the
Madagascar service.*

1

Motorship *Ferdinand de Lesseps*
Messageries Maritimes, Marseille

1969 *Delphi*

Builders: Chantiers de la Gironde,
Bordeaux
Yard no: 1
10,881 GRT; 150.0 × 19.6 m /
492 × 64.3 ft; Burmeister & Wain
diesels, Creusot; Twin screw;
12,500 BHP; 17, max 18.5 kn;
Passengers: 88 1st class, 112
tourist class, 296 3rd class.

**1951** Jul 21: Launched.
**1952** Jul: Completed.
Oct 3: Maiden voyage Marseille-
Mauritius.
**1968** Dec: Sold to C.S.
Efthymiadis, Piraeus.

**1969** Renamed *Delphi*.
Mediterranean service.
**1974** Mar 28: Arrived at
Cartagena to be broken up.

**2-4** Ferdinand de Lesseps (*2*) *came
under the Greek flag and was renamed
Delphi (3) in 1969. (4) shows the ship
after further rebuilding.*

2

3

4

Motorship *Pierre Loti*
Messageries Maritimes, Marseille

1970 *Olympia*
1972 *Patra*

Builders: Arsenal de Brest
Yard no: MD4
10,945 GRT; 150.0 × 19.6 m /
492 × 64.3 ft; Burmeister & Wain
diesels, Penhoët; Twin screw;
12,500 BHP; 17, max 18.5 kn;
Passengers: 88 1st class, 112
tourist class, 299 3rd class.

**1952** May 3: Launched.
**1953** Jun: Completed.
July 17: Maiden voyage Marseille-
Mauritius.
**1970** Sold to C.S. Efthymiadis,
Piraeus. Renamed *Olympia*.
Mediterranean service.
**1972** Renamed *Patra*.
**1973/74** Refitted as a car ferry.
**1974** May: First voyage
Patras-Brindisi for Hellenic-
Italian Line SA, a subsidiary of
Efthymiadis.

Motorship *Jean Laborde*
Messageries Maritimes, Marseille

1970 *Mykinai*
1971 *Ancona*
1974 *Eastern Princess*
1976 *Oceanos*

Builders: Chantiers de la Gironde,
Bordeaux
Yard no: 225
10,909 GRT; 150.0 × 19.6 m /
492 × 64.3 ft; Burmeister & Wain
diesels, Creusot; Twin screw;
12,500 BHP; 17, max 18.5 kn;
Passengers: 88 1st class, 112
tourist class, 299 3rd class.

**1952** Jul 12: Launched.
**1953** Jun: Completed.
Jul 31: Maiden voyage Marseille-
Mauritius.
**1970** Sold to C.S. Efthymiadis,
Piraeus. Renamed *Mykinai*.
Mediterranean service.
**1971** Renamed *Ancona*.
**1973/74** Rebuilt as a car ferry.
**1974** Transferred to the
Efthymiadis subsidiary Helite
Hellenic Lines, Panama.
Renamed *Eastern Princess*.
Sep: Piraeus-Far East, then
Singapore-Australia service.
**1976** Sold to Pontos Nav SA,
Panama. Renamed *Oceanos*.
Jul 29: Arrived at Piraeus for
repairs and refit.

*5/6 The last two vessels of the quarte*
Pierre Loti (*5*) *and* Jean Laborde (*6*).

5

6

Turbine steamer *Viet-Nam*
Messageries Maritimes, Marseille

1967 *Pacifique*
1970 *Princess Abeto*
1971 *Malaysia Baru*
1972 *Malaysia Kita*

Builders: Ch Nav de la Ciotat
Yard no: MC1
13,162 GRT; 162.1 × 22.0 m /
532 × 72.2 ft; Parsons geared
turbines, A & C Bretagne; Twin
screw; 24,000 SHP; 21, max 24.5
kn; Passengers: 117 1st class, 110
tourist class, 312 3rd class.

**1951** Oct 14: Launched.
**1952** Jul 17: Maiden voyage
Marseille-Yokohama.
**1963** 13,520 GRT.
**1967** Renamed *Pacifique*.
**1970** Sold to Cia de Nav Abeto
SA, Panama. Renamed *Princess
Abeto*. Rebuilt at Hong Kong for
pilgrim service. 1,612 passengers.
11,792 GRT.
**1971** Renamed *Malaysia Baru*. In
Fir Line service between Malaysia
and Jeddah and also Malaysia-
Singapore-India.
**1972** Renamed *Malaysia Kita*.

**1974** May 12: While lying at
Singapore for repairs a fire broke
out at 01.00 hours, the cause
unknown. It became out of control
so the ship was towed out of the
harbour and the crew taken off.
The fire took several days to burn
itself out and the *Malaysia Kita*
eventually sank in shallow water.
She was declared a total loss.
**1975** Mar 30: First attempt
(unsuccessful) to raise and salvage
the ship.
Jun 26: The wreck raised.
**1976** Apr 22: Left Singapore in
tow for Kaohsiung to be broken up.

*7/8 MM liner* Viet-Nam *(7) sailed
from 1972 as the* Malaysia Kita *in the
pilgrim service.*
*9/10 Between 1971 and 1973 (9) the*
Cambodge *(9) was refitted as the* Stella
Solaris *(10).*

Turbine steamer *Cambodge*
Messageries Maritimes, Marseille

1970 *Stella V*
1970 *Stella Solaris*

Builders: A et Ch de France,
Dunkirk
Yard no: 208
13,217 GRT; 162.1 × 22.0 m /
532 × 72.2 ft; Parsons geared
turbines, A et Ch de la Loire; Twin
screw; 24,000 SHP; 21, max 24.5
kn; Passengers: 117 1st class, 110
tourist class, 314 3rd class.

**1952** Jul 8: Launched.
**1953** Jul 31: Maiden voyage
Marseille-Yokohama.
**1963** 13,520 GRT.
**1969** Dec: Sold to Sun Line Inc,
Piraeus.
**1970** Renamed *Stella V*. Laid up
at La Spezia. Later renamed *Stella
Solaris*.
**1971** Feb: Towed to Piraeus.
Rebuilt at Perama shipyard. 750
passengers. 10,595 GRT.
**1973** Jun 25: First Mediterranean
cruise from Piraeus. Also used in
the Caribbean.

7

8

9

10

Turbine steamer *Laos*
Messageries Maritimes, Marseille

1970 *Empress Abeto*
1971 *Malaysia Raya*

Builders: Ch Nav de la Ciotat
Yard no: 170
13,212 GRT; 162.1 × 22.0 m /
532 × 72.2 ft; Parsons geared
turbines, A et Ch de la Loire; Twin
screw; 24,000 SHP; 21, max 24.5
kn; Passengers: 117 1st class, 110
tourist class, 312 3rd class.

**1952** Dec 21: Launched.
**1954** Jul 29: Maiden voyage
Marseille-Yokohama.
**1963** 13,520 GRT.
**1970** Sold to Cia de Nav Abeto
SA, Panama. Renamed *Empress
Abeto*. Rebuilt at Hong Kong for
pilgrim service. 11,792 GRT.
1,696 passengers.
**1971** Renamed *Malaysia Raya*.
In Fir Line service between
Malaysia and Jeddah and also
Malaysia-Singapore-India.
**1976** Aug 23: Totally destroyed by
fire while lying at anchor off Port

Kelang. The wreck was beached
on August 27.

Motorship *Calédonien*
Messageries Maritimes, Marseille

1972 *Nisos Kypros*
1972 *Island of Cyprus*

Builders: A et Ch de France,
Dunkirk
Yard no: 209
12,712 GRT; 167.3 × 20.6 m /
548 × 67.6 ft; Burmeister & Wain
diesels, Penhoët; Twin screw;
12,000 BHP; 17 kn; Passengers: 71
1st class, 84 tourist class, 208 3rd
class.

**1952** Apr 26: Launched.
Sep: Completed.
Oct 1: Maiden voyage Marseille-
Panama-Sydney.
**1972** Mar: Sold to C.S.
Efthymiadis, Famagusta.
Renamed *Nisos Kypros*.
Mediterranean service. In same
year renamed *Island of Cyprus*.
**1975** Broken up.

Motorship *Tahitien*
Messageries Maritimes, Marseille

1972 *Atalante*

Builders: Arsenal de Brest
Yard no: ME2
12,614 GRT; 167.3 × 20.6 m /
548 × 67.6 ft; Burmeister & Wain
diesels, Creusot; Twin screw;
12,000 BHP; 17, max 18 kn;
Passengers: 74 1st class, 84 tourist
class, 208 3rd class.

**1952** Oct 4: Launched.
**1953** May 4: Maiden voyage
Marseille-Panama-Sydney.
**1972** Sold to Aphrodite Cruises
Ltd, Limassol. Renamed *Atalante*.
Mediterranean cruises. 13,113
GRT.

11/ 12 *The third MM Far East liner
was the* Laos (*11*), *which from 1971
sailed as the* Malaysia Raya (*12*).
13/ 14 *Sister ships built for
Messageries Maritimes' Australia
service, the* Tahitien (*13*) *and*
Calédonien (*14*).

11

12

13

14

# Chargeurs Réunis Liners

Motorship *Louis Lumière*
Chargeurs Réunis, Le Havre

1967 *Mei Abeto*

Builders: Penhoët, St Nazaire
Yard no: K 14
12,358 GRT; 163.6 × 19.6 m /
537 × 64.3 ft; Sulzer diesels,
Constr Mecan; Twin screw; 12,000
BHP; 17 max 18.55 kn;
Passengers: 109 1st class, 266 2nd
class.

**1951** Nov 28: Launched.
**1952** Oct: Completed.
Hamburg-Buenos Aires service.
**1962** Transferred to Messageries
Maritimes within the SEAS.
**1964** 12,654 GRT.
**1967** Sold to Cia de Nav Abeto
SA, Panama. Renamed *Mei
Abeto*. Entered Far East-Jeddah
service.
**1976** Sold to P.T. Perusahaan
Pelajaran Arafat, Djakarta.

Motorship *Edouard Branly*
Chargeurs Réunis, Bordeaux

1957 *Antonio Pacinotti*

Builders: A et Ch de la Loire, St
Nazaire
Yard no: 352
11,298 GRT; 163.0 × 19.6 m /
535 × 64.3 ft; Sulzer diesels,
Constr Mecan; Twin screw; 11,200
BHP; 16 kn; Passengers: 91 1st
class, 52 2nd class, 398 3rd class.

**1951** Dec 5: Launched.
**1953** Feb 14: Maiden voyage
Marseille-Indo-China.
**1957** Sold to 'Italia' SAN, Genoa.
8,086 GRT after removal of
passenger accommodation.
Entered the 'Italia'
Trieste-Vancouver service.
Renamed *Antonio Pacinotti*.
**1973** Trieste-Mombasa service.

**1/2** The Louis Lumière *served in the
Hamburg-Buenos Aires service.*
**3** *The Chargeurs Réunis liner* Edouard
Branly.

1

Motorship *Henri Poincaré*
Chargeurs Réunis, Bordeaux

1957 *Galileo Ferraris*

Builders: Penhoët, St Nazaire
Yard no: L14
11,349 GRT; 163.0 × 19.6 m /
535 × 64.3 ft; Sulzer diesels,
Constr Mecan; Twin screw; 11,200
BHP; 16 kn; Passengers: 91 1st
class, 52 2nd class, 400 3rd class.

**1952**  Oct 31: Launched.
**1953**  Dec 18: Maiden voyage
Marseille-Indo-China.
**1957**  Sold to 'Italia' SAN, Genoa.
Measured at 8,101 GRT after
removal of passenger
accommodation. Renamed *Galileo
Ferraris*. Trieste-Vancouver
service.
**1973**  Trieste-Mombasa service.

Motorship *Clement Ader*
Chargeurs Réunis, Bordeaux

1957 *Alessandro Volta*

Builders: A et Ch de la Loire,
St Nazaire
Yard no: 358
11,349 GRT; 163.0 × 19.6 m /
535 × 64.3 ft; Sulzer diesels,
Constr Mecan; Twin screw; 11,200
BHP; 16 kn; Passengers: 91 1st
class, 52 2nd class, 398 3rd class.

**1953**  Jun 1: Launched.
**1954**  Apr 21: Maiden voyage
Marseille-Indo-China.
**1957**  Sold to 'Italia' SAN, Genoa.
Renamed *Alessandro Volta*. 8,086
GRT after removal of passenger
accommodation. Trieste-
Vancouver service.
**1973**  Trieste-Mombasa service.
**1974**  To Lloyd Triestino.

**4/5** Edouard Branly, Henri Poincaré
(*4*) *and* Clement Ader (*shown in* (*5*) *as*
Alessandro Volta) *were built for the
Marseille-Indo-China service.*

4

5

Motorship *City of Port Elizabeth*
Ellerman Lines, London

1971 *Mediterranean Island*
1975 *Mediterranean Sun*

Builders: Vickers-Armstrongs,
Newcastle
Yard no: 120
13,363 GRT; 164.8 × 21.7 m /
541 × 71.2 ft; Doxford diesels,
Hawthorn Leslie; Twin screw;
12,650 BHP; 16.5, max 18.8 kn;
Passengers: 107 1st class.

**1952** Mar 12: Launched.
Dec 10: Delivered.
**1953** Jan 10: Maiden voyage
London-Beira.
**1971** Sold to M.A. Karageorgis,
Piraeus. Renamed *Mediterranean
Island*. To be rebuilt at the
Perama shipyard at Piraeus for
ferry service between Patras and
Ancona. Accommodation for 850
passengers and 400 vehicles.
**1975** Refit commenced. Renamed
*Mediterranean Sun*.
Laid up.

Motorship *City of Exeter*
Ellerman Lines, London

1971 *Mediterranean Sea*

Builders: Vickers-Armstrongs,
Newcastle
Yard no: 121
13,345 GRT; 164.8 × 21.7 m /
541 × 71.2 ft; Doxford diesels,
Hawthorn Leslie; Twin screw;
12,650 BHP; 16.5, max over 18.5
kn; Passengers: 107 1st class.

**1952** Jul 7: Launched.
**1953** Apr 29: Completed.
May: Maiden voyage London-
Beira.
**1971** Sold to M.A. Karageorgis,
Piraeus. Renamed *Mediterranean
Sea*. Rebuilt for ferry service by
Perama shipyard. 15,212 GRT.
850 passengers, 400 vehicles.
**1972** Dec: First voyage
Patras-Brindisi-Ancona.
**1974** Registered at Famagusta.
16,384 GRT.
**1975** Registered under the
ownership of Mikar Ltd, Limassol.

1/2 *The* City of Port Elizabeth *(1) and*
City of Exeter *(2), built in 1953/54 for
the London-Beira service.*

Motorship *City of York*
Ellerman Lines, London

1971 *Mediterranean Sky*

Builders: Vickers-Armstrongs,
Newcastle
Yard no: 122
13,345 GRT; 164.8 × 21.7 m /
541 × 71.2 ft; Doxford diesels,
Hawthorn Leslie; Twin screw;
12,650 BHP; 16.5, max over 18.5
kn; Passengers: 107 1st class.

**1953**  Mar 30: Launched.
Oct 26: Delivered.
Nov: Maiden voyage London-
Beira.
**1971**  Sold to M.A. Karageorgis,
Piraeus. Renamed *Mediterranean
Sky*. Rebuilt at Perama shipyard
for ferry service. 14,941 GRT. 850
passengers, 400 vehicles.
**1974**  Jun: First voyage in Ancona-
Rhodes ferry service.

Motorship *City of Durban*
Ellerman Lines, London

1971 *Mediterranean Dolphin*

Builders: Vickers-Armstrongs,
Newcastle
Yard no: 123
13,343 GRT; 164.8 × 21.7 m /
541 × 71.2 ft; Doxford diesels,
Hawthorn Leslie; Twin screw;
12,650 BHP; 16.5, max 18.5 kn;
Passengers: 107 1st class.

**1953**  May 28: Launched.
**1954**  May: Completed.
London-Beira service.
**1971**  Sold to M.A. Karageorgis,
Piraeus. Renamed *Mediterranean
Dolphin*. Reconstruction planned
at Perama shipyard. 850
passengers, 400 vehicles.
**1974**  Mar 30: Arrived at
Kaohsiung to be broken up.

**3-5** *The* City of York *(3) and* City of
Durban *(4) were sold in 1971 to M.A.
Karageorgis.* (5) *shows the*
Mediterranean Sea *ex* City of Exeter.

3

Motorship *Général Mangin*
Cie de Nav Fraissinet et Cyprien
Fabre, Marseille

1969 *President*
1972 *Eastern Queen*

Builders: Penhoët, St Nazaire
Yard no: R14
12,457 GRT; 161.8 × 19.8 m /
531 × 65.0 ft; Burmeister & Wain
diesels, Penhoët; Twin screw;
9,600 BHP; 16 kn; Passengers: 132
1st class, 125 2nd class, 101 3rd
class, 500 troops; Crew: 168.

1952 Jul 9: Launched.
1953 Mar: Completed.
Marseille-Point Noire service.
1965 Transferred to Nouvelle Cie
de Paquebots, Marseille.
Continued in Congo service.
1969 Sold to Philippine President
Lines Inc, Manila.
Japan-Philippines service.

Renamed *President*.
1972 Sold to Cia de Nav Abeto
SA, Panama. Renamed *Eastern
Queen*. 11,684 GRT. Singapore-
Fremantle service for the Fir Line.
Passengers: 580 in cabins, 156 in
dormitories.

Motorship *Jean Mermoz*
Cie de Nav Fraissinet et Cyprien
Fabre, Marseille

1970 *Mermoz*

Builders: Penhoët, St Nazaire
Yard no: D17
12,460 GRT; 161.8 × 19.8 m /
531 × 65.0 ft; Burmeister &
Wain diesels, Penhoët; Twin
screw; 10,600 BHP; 16, max 18.5
kn; Passengers: 144 1st class, 140
2nd class, 110 3rd class, 460
troops; Crew: 160.

1956 Nov 17: Launched.
1957 May: Completed.
Marseille-Point Noire service.
1965 Transferred to Nouvelle Cie
de Paquebots, Marseille.
1970 Rebuilt as a cruise liner at
the Mariotti shipyards, Genoa.
757 passengers, 264 crew. 13,804
GRT. Renamed *Mermoz*.
Sep: First cruise.

*1/2 The* Général Mangin *(1) of
Nouvelle Cie de Paquebots was sold in
1969 to the Philippines to become the
President.
3/4 In 1970 the Jean Mermoz (3) was
rebuilt as the cruise liner* Mermoz *(4).*

1

2

3

4

Turbine steamer *Castel Felice*
Sitmar Line, Rome

Ex *Keren*
Ex *Kenya*
Ex *Fairstone*
Ex *Kenya*
Ex *Keren*
Ex *Kenya*
Ex *Keren*
Ex *Hydra*
Ex *Kenya*

Builders: Stephen, Glasgow
Yard no: 529
12,150 GRT; 150.3 × 19.6 m /
493 × 64.3 ft; Geared turbines
from builders; Twin screw; 9,600
SHP; 16, max 17 kn; Passengers:
596 cabin class, 944 3rd class.

**1930** Aug 27: Launched as *Kenya*
for the British India Line, London.
Dec: Completed. 9,890 GRT.
Entered Bombay-Durban service.
**1940** Served as troop transport.
Later refitted as infantry landing
ship.
**1941** Renamed *Hydra*
Oct: Renamed *Keren*.
**1946** Apr 3: Sold to Ministry of
Transport.
**1948** Aug: Laid up in Holy Loch.
**1949** Feb: Stranded after
breaking adrift in a gale.
Refloated and repaired at
Glasgow. Renamed *Kenya*. Sold to
Alva SS Co, London. Laid up at
Glasgow. Renamed *Keren* and
then *Kenya* again in the same year.
**1950** Registered in Panama for
Alva SS Co, a Sitmar subsidiary,
and renamed *Fairstone*.
Jun: Renamed *Kenya*.
Oct: Taken over by Sitmar Line
and registered in Italy.
**1951** Mar: Renamed *Keren*. To
Antwerp for rebuilding.
Aug: To Genoa for further

rebuilding.
**1952** Renamed *Castel Felice*.
12,150 GRT. 1,400 passengers in
one class.
Oct 6: First voyage Genoa-Sydney,
then Genoa-South America
service.
**1954** Jul 13: First voyage
Bremerhaven-Quebec.
**1955** Passenger accommodation
refitted at Genoa. 12,478 GRT. 28
1st class, 1,173 tourist class.
**1958** Apr 6: First voyage
Southampton-Sydney.
**1968** To Passenger Liner Service
Inc, Panama, (Sitmar). 10,952
GRT. Continued in Southampton-
Sydney service.
**1970** Oct 21: Arrived at
Kaohsiung to be broken up.

Turbine steamer *Castel Bianco*
Sitmar Line, Rome

Ex *Castelbianco*
Ex *Vassar Victory*
1957 *Begona*

Builders: Bethlehem-Fairfield,
Baltimore
Yard no: 2471
10,139 GRT; 138.7 × 18.9 m /
455 × 62.0 ft; Westinghouse
geared turbines; Single screw;
6,000 SHP; 15, max 16 kn;
Passengers: 1,200 3rd class.

**1945** May 3: Launched as *Vassar
Victory* for US Maritime
Commission.
May 28: Completed. 7,604 GRT as
cargo vessel.
**1947** Bought by Sitmar Line and
renamed *Castelbianco*. Refitted to
accommodate 480 passengers, 3rd
class.
**1952** Rebuilt at Trieste. Renamed
*Castel Bianco*. 10,139 GRT. 1,200
passengers.
**1953** Genoa-Sydney, and
Mediterranean, Central and South
America services.
**1957** Sold to Cia Trasatlantica,
Barcelona. Renamed *Begona*.
Refitted for 830 tourist class
passengers. Southampton-Spain-
Central America service.
**1974** Sep 27: The *Begona* left
Southampton for the West Indies
with 800 passengers. On October 3
she put into Teneriffe with engine
trouble but was able to continue
her voyage the next day after
repairs. In the Atlantic she broke
down completely and after drifting
helplessly for a few days was towed
to Bridgetown by the German tug
*Oceanic*, arriving on October 17.
Dec 24: Arrived at Castellon, having
been sold for scrapping there.

1

2

**1** *Sitmar Line's* Castel Felice.
**2** *The* Castel Bianco *was a conversion from a 'Victory'-type cargo vessel.*

Turbine steamer *Aquarama*
Michigan-Ohio Nav Co,
Wilmington

Ex *Marine Star*

Builders: Sun SB & DD Co,
Chester
Yard no: 357
12,773 GRT; 159.3 × 21.8 m /
523 × 72.0 ft; Geared turbines,
General Electric Co.; Single screw;
9,900 SHP; 17 kn; Passengers:
2,500; Crew: 190.

**1945** Built as C4-cargo vessel
*Marine Star* for the US Maritime
Commission, Philadelphia. 10,780
GRT.
**1952** Sold to the Sand Products
Corporation, Wilmington. Rebuilt
as a ferry by Todd, Brooklyn, and
by West Michigan Dock & Market
Corp. Renamed *Aquarama*.
**1955** Sep: Reconstruction
completed.
**1956** Sep: First voyage Detroit-
Cleveland on Lake Erie. On this
short run 2,500 deck passengers
and 165 cars can be
accommodated.

Diesel-electric vessel *Aurelia*
Cogedar Line, Genoa

Ex *Beaverbrae*
Ex *Huascaran*
1970 *Romanza*

Builders: Blohm & Voss,
Hamburg
Yard no: 518
10,022 GRT; 148.7 × 18.4 m /
488 × 60.4 ft; MAN diesels from
builders, generators and driving
motors from Siemens-Schuckert;
Single screw; 6,400 BHP; 17 kn;
Passengers: 1,124 in one class.

**1938** Dec 15: Launched as cargo
and passenger vessel *Huascaran*
for Hamburg-America Line.
**1939** Apr 27: Delivered. 6,951
GRT. 32 1st class passengers.
Hamburg-America service
between Hamburg and the west
coast of South America.
**1940** Repair ship in the German
Navy.
**1945** Nov 14: Handed over to the
Canadian government. Managed
by Park SS Co.
**1947** Sep 2: Sold to Canadian
Pacific, Montreal. Refitted at
Sorel, Quebec, to accommodate
775 passengers. 9,034 GRT.
**1948** Feb 7: Renamed
*Beaverbrae*.
Feb 8: First voyage St John-
Bremerhaven. Emigrant service.
**1951** St John-Bremen service.
**1954** Nov 1: Sold to Cogedar Line.
Renamed *Aurelia*. Rebuilt at
Monfalcone for 1,124 tourist class
passengers.
**1955** May 13: First voyage Trieste-
Sydney. 10,022 GRT.
Nov 15: First voyage
Genoa-Sydney. 10,022 GRT.
Nov 15: First voyage
Genoa-Sydney.

**1958/59** Further rebuilding.
work. New MAN diesels, 10,480
GRT.
**1959** Jun 12: First voyage
Bremerhaven-Sydney.
**1964** Dec 9: First voyage
Rotterdam-Australia/New
Zealand.
**1968** Passenger accommodation
refitted. Now 740 in one class.
Southampton-Madeira service.
Cruising.
**1970** Sold to the Chandris group.
Sep: Renamed *Romanza*.
Registered at Piraeus under the
ownership of International Cruises
SA.
**1971** Cruising after refit at
Piraeus. 8,891 GRT.

**3** *The Great Lakes car ferry*
Aquarama.
**4** *The* Aurelia *was rebuilt for the
emigrant service to Australia.*

3

4

Turbine steamer *Fairsky*
Fairline Shipping Corp, Monrovia

Ex *Castel Forte*
Ex *Attacker*
Ex *Barnes*
Ex *Steel Artisan*
1959 *Fair Sky*

Builders: Western Pipe & Steel
Co, San Francisco
Yard no: 62
12,464 GRT; 153.0 × 21.2 m /
502 × 69.5 ft; Geared turbines,
General Electric Co; Single screw;
8,500 SHP; 17.5 kn; Passengers:
1,461 in one class.

**1941** Sep 27: Launched as
C3-cargo vessel *Steel Artisan*.
Taken over by the US Navy.
Continued under construction as
auxiliary aircraft carrier *Barnes*.
**1942** Sep 30: Handed over to the
Royal Navy as HMS *Attacker* on
completion.
**1946** Jan 5: Handed back to the
US Navy. Laid up.
**1952** Sold to Sitmar Line, Rome.
Reconstructed as cargo vessel.
7,800 GRT. Renamed *Castel Forte*.
**1957** Feb: Work commenced on
conversion to passenger ship.
Later moved to Genoa.
**1958** Renamed *Fairsky*.
Registered in Monrovia for
Fairline, a Sitmar company.
Jun 28: First voyage Southampton-
Sydney.
**1959** Renamed *Fair Sky*.

Turbine steamer *Monterey*
Matson Nav Co, San Francisco

Ex *Free State Mariner*

Builders: Bethlehem SB Corp,
Sparrow's Point
Yard no: 4507
14,799 GRT; 171.1 × 23.2 m /
561 × 76.1 ft; Geared turbines
from builders; Single screw;
19,250 SHP; 20, max 22 kn;
Passengers: 365 1st class; Crew:
274.

**1952** May 29: Launched for US
Maritime Commission as C4-cargo
vessel *Free State Mariner*.
Dec 8: Delivered.
**1955** Sold to Matson.
**1956** Rebuilt as a passenger ship
by Williamette Iron & Steel Corp,
Portland, Oregon. Renamed
*Monterey*.
**1957** Jan 8: First voyage San
Francisco-Honolulu-Auckland-
Sydney.
**1971** Jan: Sold to Pacific Far East
Line Inc, San Francisco. Cruising
in the Pacific.

Turbine steamer *Mariposa*
Matson Nav Co, San Francisco

Ex *Pine Tree Mariner*

Builders: Bethlehem Steel Co,
Quincy
Yard no: 1624
14,812 GRT; 171.1 × 23.2 m /
561 × 76.1 ft; Geared turbines
from builders; Single screw;
19,250 SHP; 20, max 22 kn;
Passengers: 365 1st class; Crew:
274.

**1952** Nov 7: Launched as cargo
vessel *Pine Tree Mariner* for US
Maritime Commission.
**1953** Apr 3: Delivered. 9,217
GRT.
**1956** Sold to Matson Nav Co.
**1956** Rebuilt as a passenger ship
by Williamette Iron & Steel Corp,
Portland. Renamed *Mariposa*.
Oct 27:Maiden voyage San
Francisco-Honolulu-Auckland-
Sydney.
**1971** Jan: Sold to Pacific Far East
Line Inc, San Francisco. Cruising
in the Pacific.

**5** *The* Fairsky *was rebuilt for the
passenger service to Australia.*

5

**6/7** *The liners* Monterey *and*
Mariposa, *converted from C4-cargo
vessels for Matson Line. The latter is
shown in (4) in the colours of the
Pacific Far East Line.*

Turbine steamer *Atlantic*
American Banner Lines, New
York

Ex *Badger Mariner*
1971 *Universe Campus*
1976 *Universe*

Builders: Sun SB DD Co, Chester
Yard no: 586
14,138 GRT; 171.9 × 23.2 m /
564 × 76.1 ft; Geared turbines,
General Electric Co; Single screw;
20,000 SHP; 20, max 24 kn;
Passengers: 40 1st class, 860
tourist class; Crew: 320.

**1953** Jul 1: Launched as C4-cargo
vessel *Badger Mariner* for the US
Maritime Commission.
Oct 29: Delivered. 9,214 GRT.
**1957** Sold to American Banner

Lines. Renamed *Atlantic*. Rebuilt
as a passenger ship by Ingalls SB
Corp, Pascagoula.
**1958** Jun 11: First voyage New
York-Amsterdam.
**1959** Oct 25: Last voyage
Amsterdam-New York.
Sold to American Export Lines,
New York. Refitted for
Mediterranean service by Sun SB
Co, Chester.
**1960** May 16: First voyage New
York-Haifa.
**1965** Apr: 840 passengers in one
class.
**1967** Oct 13: Laid up at New
York. From March 1969 at
Baltimore.
**1971** Sold to the C.Y. Tung
group. Renamed *Universe*

*Campus*. Registered in Monrovia
for Seawise Foundations Inc.
13,950 GRT.
Sep 4: First cruise from Los
Angeles.
**1976** Renamed *Universe*.
Jul 24: Laid up at San Francisco.

**8** *The* Universe Campus *ex* Atlantic.

8

Motorship *Kungsholm*
Swedish America Line,
Gothenburg

1965 *Europa*

Builders: 'De Schelde', Vlissingen
Yard no: 273
21,141 GRT; 182.9 × 23.5 m /
600 × 77.1 ft; Burmeister & Wain
diesels; Twin screw; 18.600 BHP;
19, max 21.2 m; Passengers: 176
1st class, 626 tourist class; Crew:
418.

**1952** Oct 18: Launched.
**1953** Oct 9: Completed.
Nov 24: Maiden voyage
Gothenburg-New York.
**1964** Sold to North German
Lloyd, Bremen, with delivery set
for 1965.
**1965** Oct 16: Taken over by NGL.
Renamed *Europa*.
**1966** Jan 9: First voyage
Bremerhaven-New York. 21,514
GRT. Passengers: 122 1st class,
721 tourist class.

**1970** Sep 1: Hamburg-America
and North German Lloyd Lines
amalgamated to form
Hapag-Lloyd AG.
**1972** Used exclusively for
cruising.

*1/2 The* Europa *(1) ex* Kungsholm *has
been sailing with a white hull since
1972.*

1

2

Motorship *Gripsholm*
Swedish America Line,
Gothenburg

1974 *Navarino*

Builders: Ansaldo, Sestri-Ponente
Yard no: 1500
23,191 GRT; 192.3 × 24.9 m /
631 × 81.7 ft; Götaverken-diesels;
Twin screw; 18,800 BHP; 19, max
21 kn; Passengers: 150 1st class,
692 tourist class; Crew: 364.

**1956** Apr 8: Launched.
**1957** Apr: Completed.
May 14: Maiden voyage
Gothenburg-New York.
**1966** 23,216 GRT. 22,725 GRT in

1972. Used mainly for cruising.
**1974** Nov: To M.A. Karageorgis,
Piraeus. Renamed *Navarino*.

3

**3/4** *The* Gripsholm *came into service in 1957.*

# The Olympia

Turbine steamer *Olympia*
Greek Line, Monrovia

Builders: Stephen, Glasgow
Yard no: 636
22,979 GRT; 186.5 × 24.1 m /
612 × 79.0 ft; Parsons geared
turbines from builders; Twin
screw; 25,000 SHP; 21, max 23 kn;
Passengers: 138 1st class, 1,169
tourist class.

**1953** Apr 16: Launched unnamed.
Oct 12: Named and delivered.
Registered under the ownership of
the Transatlantic Shipping Corp,
Monrovia.
Oct 15: Maiden voyage Glasgow-
Liverpool-New York, after having
made a private cruise to Dublin.
Nov 17: First voyage Bremerhaven-
New York.
**1955** Mar 26: First voyage New
York-Piraeus. 17,362 GRT.
**1961** Service extended to Haifa.
**1968** Registered at Andros under
the Greek flag. 17,434 GRT.

**1970** Cruising exclusively.
**1974** Mar 24: Laid up at Piraeus.

1 *The Greek liner* Olympia.

Motorship *Uige*
Cia Colonial, Lisbon

Builders: Cockerill, Hoboken
Yard no: 769
10,001 GRT; 145.4 × 19.2 m /
477 × 63.0 ft; Burmeister & Wain
diesels from builders; Single
screw; 6,850 BHP; 16 kn;
Passengers: 78 1st class, 493 3rd
class.

**1954** Jan 23: Launched.
Jul 7: Delivered.
Lisbon-Mozambique service.
**1976** Jan 27: Laid up at Lisbon.

Motorship *Niassa*
Cia Nacional, Lisbon

Builders: Cockerill, Hoboken
Yard no: 768
10,912 GRT; 151.5 × 19.5 m /
497 × 64.0 ft; Doxford diesels,
Ansaldo; Single screw; 7,150 BHP;
16 kn; Passengers: 22 1st class,
284 tourist class.

**1955** Mar 5: Launched.
Aug: Completed.
Lisbon-Mòssamedes service.
**1959** 10,742 GRT.
**1974** The owners' name was
changed to Cia Portuguesa de
Transp Maritimos through
amalgamation with Carregadores
Acoreanos and Empresa Insulana.

*1/2 The motorships* Uige *(1) and*
Niassa *(2) were built for service
between Lisbon and Africa.*

1

2

Turbine steamer *Saxonia*
Cunard Line, Liverpool

1962 *Carmania*
1973 *Leonid Sobinov*

Builders: Brown, Clydebank
Yard no: 692
21,637 GRT; 185.3 × 24.5 m /
497 × 80.4 ft; Geared turbines
from builders; Twin screw; 24,500
SHP; 20, max over 22 kn;
Passengers: 110 1st class, 819
tourist class; Crew: 461.

**1954** Feb 17: Launched.
**1954** Aug: Completed.
Sep 2: Maiden voyage Liverpool-
Montreal.
**1957** Jun 19: First voyage
Southampton-Montreal.
**1961** Apr: First voyage Liverpool-
New York.
**1962/63** Refitted at Clydebank by
Brown. 22,592 GRT. Renamed
*Carmania*. Hull and
superstructure painted bright
green. Passengers: 117 1st class,
764 tourist class.
**1963** Apr 8: First voyage
Rotterdam-Montreal. Cruising
from US ports in winter.
**1967** White hull. Cruising only.
**1969** 21,370 GRT.
**1971** Oct: Laid up. Put up for sale
in December.
**1973** Aug: Sold to Nikreis
Maritime Corp, Panama, which
acquired the ship for the Soviet
state shipping company. Renamed
*Leonid Sobinov*.
**1974** Feb 25: First voyage
Southampton-Sydney, followed by
cruising in Australasian and Far
East waters.

Turbine steamer *Ivernia*
Cunard Line, Liverpool

1963 *Franconia*
1973 *Fedor Shalyapin*

Builders: Brown, Clydebank
Yard no: 693
21,717 GRT; 185.3 × 24.5 m /
608 × 80.4 ft; Geared turbines
from builders; Twin screw; 24,500
SHP; 20, max over 22 kn;
Passengers: 110 1st class, 833
tourist class; Crew: 461.

**1954** Dec 14: Launched.
**1955** Jun: Completed.
Jul 1: Maiden voyage Greenock-
Montreal.
Jul 27: First voyage Liverpool-
Montreal.
**1957** Apr 17: First voyage
Southampton-Montreal.
**1962** Oct: Refitted by Brown, the
work lasting until June 1963. New
passenger accommodation. 119 1st
class, 728 tourist class. 22,637
GRT. Painted green.
**1963** Jan 1: Renamed *Franconia*.
Jul: First voyage Rotterdam-
Montreal.
**1967** Painted white.
**1969** 21,406 GRT.
**1970** Cruising only.
**1971** Oct: Laid up. Put up for sale
in December.
**1973** Aug: Sold to Nikreis
Maritime Corporation, Panama,
which acquired the ship for the
Soviet state shipping company.
Nov 20: First voyage under the
name *Fedor Shalyapin* from
Southampton to Sydney and
Auckland. Subsequently cruising
in Australasian and Far East
waters.

**1-3** *The* Carmania *ex* Saxonia *painted
green after her 1962/63 refit (1) and as
a white cruise liner from 1967 (2). (3),
the* Ivernia *shows the original
appearance of this class.*

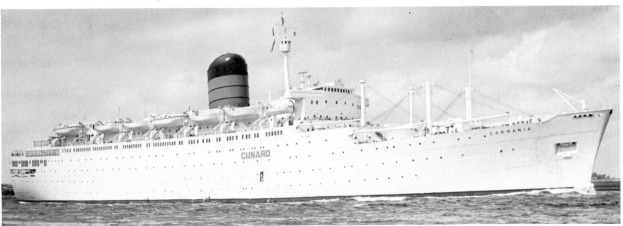

Turbine steamer *Carinthia*
Cunard Line, Liverpool

1968 *Fairland*
1971 *Fairsea*

Builders: Brown, Clydebank
Yard no: 699
21,947 GRT; 185.3 × 24.5 m /
608 × 80.4 ft; Geared turbines
from builders; Twin screw; 24,500
SHP; 20, max over 22 kn;
Passengers: 154 1st class, 714
tourist class; Crew: 461.

**1955** Dec 14: Launched.
**1956** Jun: Completed.
Jun 27: Maiden voyage Liverpool-
Montreal. Liverpool-New York
service in winter.
**1967** Painted white. Cruising
only.
**1968** Jan: Sold to Fairland
Shipping Corp, Monrovia.
Renamed *Fairland*. The ship was
intended for the Sitmar Line's
Southampton-New Zealand
service, but was laid up at
Southampton.
**1970** Feb 21: Arrived at Trieste
and refitted as cruise liner. 21,916
GRT.
**1971** Renamed *Fairsea*.

Registered in Monrovia under the
ownership of The Fairsea
Shipping Corp.
**1972** Jul: Back in service after
rebuilding as a cruise liner for 884
passengers. 16,627 GRT. Cruising
from US ports.

Turbine steamer *Sylvania*
Cunard Line, Liverpool

1968 *Fairwind*

Builders: Brown, Clydebank
Yard no: 700
21,989 GRT; 185.3 × 24.5 m /
608 × 80.4 ft; Geared turbines
from builders; Twin screw; 24,500
SHP; 20, max over 22 kn;
Passengers: 154 1st class, 724
tourist class; Crew: 461.

**1956** Nov 22: Launched.
**1957** Jun: Completed.
Jun 5: Maiden voyage Greenock-
Montreal.
Jun 26: First voyage Liverpool-
Montreal. Liverpool-New York
service in winter.
**1965** 22,017 GRT.
**1967** Painted white. Cruising
only.
**1968** Sold to the Fairwind
Shipping Corp, Monrovia.
Renamed *Fairwind*. Intended for
Sitmar Line's Southampton-New
Zealand service, but laid up.
**1970** Jan 14: Arrived at Trieste.
Rebuilt for cruising. 21,985 GRT.
**1972** 16,667 GRT. Cruising from
American ports.

4

**4** *The* Fedor Shalyapin *ex* Ivernia.
**5/6** *The sister ships* Carinthia (5) *and*
Sylvania (6) *were built for the Canada
service.*
**7** *The* Fairwind *ex* Sylvania.

5

6

7

Motorship *Brazil Maru*
Osaka Shosen KK, Osaka

Builders: Mitsubishi, Kobe
Yard no: 858
10,100 GRT; 155.4 × 19.6 m /
510 × 64.3 ft; Sulzer diesels from
builders; Single screw; 9,000 BHP;
16.5, max 20.3 kn; Passengers: 12
1st class, 68 tourist class, 902 3rd
class.

**1954** Apr 6: Launched.
Jul 10: Delivered.
Kobe-Buenos Aires service.
**1963** Dec: Osaka Shosen KK
amalgamated with Mitsui Line to
form Mitsui-OSK Line.
**1965** Passenger accommodation
refitted. 12 cabin class, 348 tourist
class. 10,216 GRT.
Oct 30: First voyage Kobe-South
America-North American West
Coast.
**1973** Mar 6: Laid up at Kobe.
Sep: One cruise to Shanghai, then
sold to Toba Brazil Maru KK.
**1974** Refitted as museum and
restaurant ship by Mitsubishi at
Kobe. Stationed at Toba in Ise
Bay.
Jul 5: Official opening.

Turbine steamer *Argentina Maru*
Osaka Shosen KK, Osaka

1972 *Nippon Maru*

Builders: Mitsubishi, Kobe
Yard no: 898
10,864 GRT; 156.6 × 20.4 m /
514 × 66.9 ft; Westinghouse
geared turbines from builders;
Single screw; 9,000 SHP; 16.5,
max 19.5 kn; Passengers: 12 1st
class, 82 2nd class, 960 3rd class.

**1958** Feb 8: Launched.
Jun 2: Maiden voyage in Japan-
Buenos Aires service.
**1963** Dec: Osaka Shosen
amalgamated with Mitsui Line to
form Mitsui-OSK Line.
**1965** Passenger accommodation
refitted. 23 cabin class, 352 tourist
class. 10,770 GRT.
Aug 30: First voyage Japan-South
America-North American West
Coast.
**1972** Feb: Used only for cruising.
Renamed *Nippon Maru*.
**1976** Dec 20: Arrived at
Kaohsiung to be broken up.

1

1 *The* Brazil Maru *entered service in
1954, the first post-war Japanese
ocean-going passenger ship.*
2/3 *The* Argentina Maru *(2) was
renamed* Nippon Maru *(3) in 1972.*

# Shaw Savill Liners

Turbine steamer *Southern Cross*
Shaw, Savill & Albion,
Southampton

1973 *Calypso*

Builders: Harland & Wolff,
Belfast
Yard no: 1498
20,204 GRT; 184.0 × 23.9 m /
604 × 78.4 ft; Geared turbines
from builders; Twin screw; 20,000
SHP; 20, max 21 kn; Passengers:
1,160 tourist class.

**1954** Aug 17: Launched.
**1955** Feb 23: Delivered.
Mar 29: Maiden voyage in round-
the-world service from
Southampton.
**1968** 19,313 GRT.
**1971** Jun 30: Cruising from
Liverpool.
Nov: Laid up at Southampton,
from 1972 in River Fal.
**1973** Jan: Sold to Cia de Vap
Cerulea SA, Ithaka. Renamed
*Calypso*.
Mar: Arrived at Piraeus. Refitted
as cruise liner. 16,500 GRT.

**1975** Apr 25: First Mediterranean
cruise from Piraeus.
Jun: Cruising from Tilbury or
Southampton for Thomson
cruises.

Turbine steamer *Northern Star*
Shaw, Savill & Albion,
Southampton

Builders: Vickers-Armstrongs,
Southampton
Yard no: 175
24,733 GRT; 198.1 × 25.5 m /
650 × 83.6 ft; Parsons geared
turbines; Twin screw; 22,000 SHP;
19.5, max 22 kn; Passengers:
1,412 tourist class; Crew: 490.

**1961** Jun 27: Launched.
**1962** Jun 26: Completed.
Jul 10: Maiden voyage in
Southampton-round-the-world
service.
**1968** 23,983 GRT.
**1974** Dec 1: Arrived at
Kaohsiung to be broken up by Li
Chong Steel & Iron Works.

**1** *The profile of the* Southern Cross
*was revolutionary when she entered
service in 1955. For the first time, the
engines and funnel of a large
passenger liner had been sited aft.*
**2/3** *In 1962 the* Northern Star *entered
the round-the-world service.*

1

Motorship *Cabo San Roque*
Ybarra y Cia, Saville

Builders: Soc Española de
Construccion Naval, Bilbao
Yard no: 75
14,491 GRT; 169.7 × 21.1 m /
557 × 69.2 ft; Sulzer diesels from
builders; Twin screw; 14,600
BHP; 20, max 22 kn; Passengers:
241 cabin class, 582 tourist class;
Crew: 231.

**1955** Apr 23: Launched.
**1957** Aug: Completed.
Genoa-Buenos Aires service.
Cruising.
**1972** 14,182 GRT.

Motorship *Cabo San Vicente*
Ybarra y Cia, Seville

Builders: Soc Española de
Construccion Naval, Bilbao
Yard no: 76
14,569 GRT; 169.7 × 21.1 m /
557 × 69.2 ft; Sulzer diesels from
builders; Twin screw; 14,600
BHP; 20, max 22 kn; Passengers:
241 cabin class, 582 tourist class;
Crew: 231.

**1956** Oct 6: Launched.
**1959** Apr: Completed.
Genoa-Buenos Aires service.
Cruising.
**1972** 14,153 GRT.

**1975** Nov: Sold to Mogul Line
Ltd, Bombay. Renamed *Noor
Jehan*. Pilgrim voyages.

**1-3** *The sister ships* Cabo San Roque,
*(1) and (2) and* Cabo San Vicente *(3).*

1

2

3

**The Reina del Mar**

Turbine steamer *Reina del Mar*
Pacific Steam Nav Co, Liverpool

Builders: Harland & Wolff,
Belfast
Yard no: 1533
20,234 GRT; 183.2 × 23.9 m /
601 × 78.4 ft; Parsons geared
turbines, H & W; Twin screw;
17,000 SHP; 18 kn; Passengers:
207 1st class, 216 cabin class, 343
tourist class; Crew: 327.

**1955** Jun 7: Launched.
**1956** Apr: Completed.
May 3: Maiden voyage Liverpool-
Valparaiso.
**1963** Chartered to the Travel
Savings Association.
**1964** Mar 10: Rebuilding as
cruise liner commenced by
Harland & Wolff. 21,501 GRT.

1,047 passengers in one class.
Jun 10: First voyage to New
York for the Travel Savings
Association, the ship being under
the management of the Union-
Castle Line.
Nov: The *Reina del Mar* was
painted in Union-Castle colours.
She was used solely for cruising,
from Southampton in summer
and from Cape Town in winter.
**1967** 20,750 GRT.
**1973** Sep: Sold by the Pacific
Steam Nav Co (Royal Mail Lines),
to the Union-Castle Line.
**1975** Jul 30: Arrived at
Kaohsiung to be broken up by
Tung Cheng Steel Manufacturing
Co.

**1/2** *Built for the Valparaiso service of
the PSN Co, the* Reina del Mar *was
sold to the Union-Castle Line (2) in
1973.*

1

Turbine steamer *Empress of Britain*
Canadian Pacific, London

1964 *Queen Anna Maria*
1975 *Carnivale*

Builders: Fairfield, Glasgow
Yard no: 731
25,516 GRT; 195.1 × 26.0 m /
640 × 85.3 ft; Geared turbines
from builders; Twin screw; 30,000
SHP; 20, max 21 kn; 160 1st class,
894 tourist class; Crew: 464.

**1955** Jun 22: Launched.
**1956** Mar 9-10: Trials.
Apr 20: Maiden voyage
Liverpool-Montreal. She had
previously made two short cruises.
**1964** Feb: Sold to the Greek Line
(Transoceanic Nav Corp), in
Andros.
Nov 16: Handed over.
Nov 18: Renamed *Queen Anna
Maria*.
Refitted at the Mariotti shipyards,
Genoa, the work lasting from
November 1964 to March 6 1965.
21,716 GRT. Passengers: 168 1st
class; 1,145 tourist class; 741
while cruising.

**1965** Mar 24: First voyage
Piraeus-New York. Haifa-New
York service. Cruising.
**1975** Jan 22: Laid up at Piraeus.
Dec: To Carnival Cruise Lines
Inc, Panama. Renamed
*Carnivale*.
**1976** Feb: First cruise in the
Caribbean.

Turbine steamer *Empress of
England*
Canadian Pacific, London

1970 *Ocean Monarch*

Builders: Vickers-Armstrongs,
Newcastle
Yard no: 155
25,585 GRT; 195.0 × 26.0 m /
640 × 85.3 ft; Geared turbines
from builders; Twin screw; 30,000
SHP; 20, max 21 kn; Passengers:
160 1st class, 898 tourist class;
Crew: 464.

**1956** May 9: Launched.
**1957** Mar 19: Delivered.
Apr 18: Maiden voyage
Liverpool-Montreal.
**1970** Feb: Sold to Shaw, Savill &
Albion, Southampton. Renamed
*Ocean Monarch*.
Apr 11: One voyage Liverpool-
Southampton-Australia, then
refitted as one-class cruise liner by
Cammell Laird. 1,372 passengers.
25,971 GRT.
**1971** Oct 16: First cruise
Southampton-Mediterranean.
**1975** Jul 17: Arrived at
Kaohsiung to be broken up.

1/2 *The* Empress of Britain *(1) went to
Greece in 1964 to become the* Queen
Anna Maria *(2).*
3/4 *Shaw Savill bought the* Empress of
England *(3) in 1970, and placed her in
service as the* Ocean Monarch *(4).*

1

2

3

4

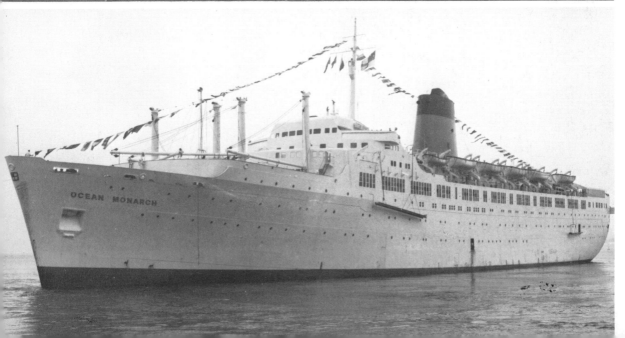

Turbine steamer *Empress of Canada*
Canadian Pacific, London

1972 *Mardi Gras*

Builders: Vickers-Armstrongs,
Newcastle
Yard no: 171
27,284 GRT; 198.1 × 26.4 m /
650 × 86.6 ft; Parsons geared
turbines from builders; Twin
screw; 30,000 SHP; 20, max 23
kn; Passengers: 192 1st class, 856
tourist class; Crew: 470.

**1960** May 10: Launched.
**1961** Mar 7: Trials.
Mar 29: Delivered.
Apr 24: Maiden voyage Liverpool-
Montreal.
**1972** Jan: Sold to Carnival Cruise
Lines Inc, Panama. Renamed
*Mardi Gras*. 18,261 GRT.

Feb 26: First cruise from Tilbury
to Miami.

5-7 *The* Empress of Canada. *In (7) sh*
*is shown in the new Canadian Pacific*
*colours.*

5

# Nevasa and Oxfordshire

Turbine steamer *Nevasa*
British India Line, London

Builders: Barclay, Curle & Co,
London
Yard no: 733
20,527 GRT; 185.6 × 23.8 m /
609 × 78.1 ft; Parsons geared
turbines from builders; Twin
screw; 20,280 SHP; 17, max over
21 kn; Passengers: 220 1st class,
100 2nd class, 180 3rd class, 1,000
troops; Crew: 409.

**1955** Nov 30: Launched.
**1956** Jul 12: Delivered.
The *Nevasa* was built as a troop
transport for service between
Great Britain and her overseas
possessions. The Ministry of
Transport bore a share of the
cost.
**1962** Oct 13: Laid up in River
Fal.
**1963** The Ministry of Transport
terminated the 15 years charter
and handed the *Nevasa* over to the
British India Line to use as they
wished.
**1964/65** Rebuilt by Silley, Cox &
Co for scholars' cruises. 20,746
GRT. 307 passengers in cabins,
783 in dormitories.
**1965** Oct 28: First scholars' cruise
from Southampton.
**1970** 20,160 GRT.
**1972** The British India Line's
ships were transferred to P & O.
**1975** Mar 30: The *Nevasa* arrived
at Kaohsiung, where she was
broken up.

Turbine steamer *Oxfordshire*
Bibby Line, Liverpool

1964 *Fairstar*

Builders: Fairfield, Glasgow
Yard no: 775
20,586 GRT; 186.9 × 23.8 m /
613 × 78.1 ft; Parsons geared
turbines, Fairfield; Twin screw;
18,000 SHP; 17, max 21 kn;
Passengers: 220 1st class, 100 2nd
class, 180 3rd class, 1,000 troops,
Crew: 409.

**1955** Dec 15: Launched.
**1957** Feb 13: Delivered.
The *Oxfordshire* was built as a
troop transport for service
between Great Britain and her
overseas possessions. The Ministry
of Transport bore a share of the
cost.
**1962** The government ended the
contract at the end of the year and
placed the ship at the disposal of
the Bibby Line.
**1963** Chartered to the Fairline
Shipping Corp (Sitmar) for six
years.
May 20: Arrived at Schiedam to
be rebuilt by Wilton-Fijenoord for
the Australia service.
**1964** Mar: The Fairstair Shipping
Corp, Monrovia, bought the ship
and renamed her *Fairstar*.
Apr: Because of a disagreement
with the shipyard the work was
completed at Southampton by
Harland & Wolff.
May: 21,619 GRT after
reconstruction. 1,870 passengers
in one class.
May 19: First voyage
Southampton-Brisbane.
**1973** Aug 20: First cruise from
Sydney. Used only for cruising.

1 *The* Nevasa *was built as a troop
transport with the financial
participation of the Ministry of
Transport.*
2/3 *The* Oxfordshire *(2) also sailed a
a troop transport for the MoT and w
sold to the Sitmar group in 1964 to
become the* Fairstar *(3).*

1

2

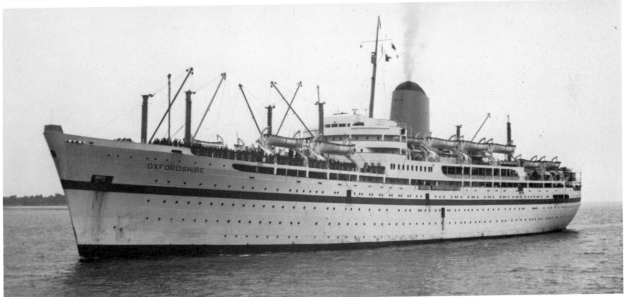

3

# The Bergensfjord

Motorship *Bergensfjord*
Norwegian America Line

1972 *De Grasse*
1973 *Rasa Sayang*

Builders: Swan, Hunter &
Wigham Richardson, Newcastle
Yard no: 1849
18,739 GRT; 176.2 × 22.0 m /
578 × 72.2 ft; Stork diesels; Twin
screw; 18,600 BHP; 20, max
23.84 kn; Passengers: 103 1st
class, 775 tourist class; Crew: 335.

**1955** Jul 18: Launched.
**1956** May 14: Delivered.
May 30: Maiden voyage Oslo-New
York.
**1971** Sold to CGT, Dunkirk, as
replacement for the *Antilles*.
Renamed *De Grasse*. The name
*Louisiane* had first been
suggested.

**1973** Sep: Sale under negotiation
to Coral Riviera Ltd, Tel Aviv,
which wanted to use the ship, to
be renamed *Coral Riviera*, for
cruising in the Far East under the
Panama flag. The deal fell
through.
Instead, the *De Grasse* was sold to
Thoresen & Co, Hong Kong.
Nov: Renamed *Rasa Sayang*.
**1974** Jan: Arrived at Singapore
and registered there.

**1/2** *The* Bergensfjord *(1) sailed from
1971 to 1973 as the* De Grasse *for
CGT.*
**3** *The* Rasa Sayang *in Malta in
December 1973.*

1

2

3

# Jadotville and Baudouinville

Turbine Steamer *Jadotville*
Compagnie Maritime Belge,
Antwerp

1961 *Chitral*

Builders: Penhoët, St Nazaire
Yard no: 516
13,724 GRT; 169.8 × 21.4 m /
557 × 70.2 ft; Parsons geared
turbines from builders; Single
screw; 12,500 SHP; 16.5 max 18
kn; Passengers: 300 in one class;
Crew: 196.

**1955** Nov 30: Launched.
**1956** Jun 17-19. Trials.
Jul 8: Delivered.
Jul 23: Maiden voyage Antwerp-
Matadi .
**1961** Jan: Sold to P & O Line,
London. Renamed *Chitral*.
Passenger accommodation altered:
231 in one class. 13,821 GRT.
Mar 2: First voyage London-
Yokohama.
**1970** To Eastern & Australian SS
Co, London. Service between Far
East and Australia.
**1975** To Taiwan to be broken up.

Turbine steamer *Baudouinville*
Compagnie Maritime Belge,
Antwerp

1961 *Cathay*

Builders: Cockerill, Hoboken
Yard no: 778
13,922 GRT; 170.5 × 21.4 m /
559 × 70.2 ft; Geared turbines
from builders; Single screw;
12,500 SHP; 16.5, max 18 kn;
Passengers: 301 in one class;
Crew: 196.

**1957** Jan 10: Launched.
Oct 17-19: Trials.
Nov 2: Maiden voyage Antwerp-
Matadi.
**1961** Jan: Sold to P & O Line,
London. Renamed *Cathay*. 231
passengers in one class. 13,809
GRT.
Apr 14: First voyage London-
Yokohama.
**1969** 13,531 GRT.
**1970** To Eastern & Australian SS
Co, London. Entered service
between Far East and Australia.
**1976** Jan: Sold to the People's
Republic of China.

1-3 *The sister ships* Jadotville (*1*) *and*
Baudouinville *were sold to P & O in
1961 to become the* Chitral (*2*) *and*
Cathay (*3*).

1

2

3

Turbine steamer *Dinteldyk*
Holland-America Line,
Rotterdam

1970 *Oriental Fantasia*
1972 *Hongkong Success*

Builders: Wilton-Fijenoord,
Schiedam
Yard no: 752
11,366 GRT; 153.7 × 21.1 m /
504 × 69.2 ft; Geared turbines
from builders; Twin screw; 9,350
SHP; 16.5, max 17.5 kn;
Passengers: 60 in one class.

**1956** Jun 9: Launched.
**1957** Feb 27: Completed.
Mar: Maiden voyage.
Hamburg-Vancouver service.
**1970** Sold to the C.Y. Tung
group. Registered as *Oriental
Fantasia* under the ownership of
the Oriental Central American
Line, Monrovia. 10,417 GRT.
Transpacific service.
**1972** Sold to the Pacific Union
Line Ltd, Hong Kong. Renamed
*Hongkong Success*. Far East-
Australia service.

Turbine steamer *Statendam*
Holland-America Line, Rotterdam

Builders: Wilton-Fijenoord,
Schiedam
Yard no: 753
24,294 GRT; 195.8 × 24.7 m /
642 × 81.0 ft; Parsons geared
turbines from builders; Twin
screw; 22,000 SHP; 19, max 21.9
kn; Passengers: 84 1st class, 867
tourist class; Crew: 437.

**1956** Jun 12: Floated in building
dock, unnamed.
Dec 15: Trials. Towed back to
shipyard because of engine
breakdown.
**1957** Jan 23: Named *Statendam*
at sea during delivery voyage.
Feb 6: Maiden voyage Rotterdam-
New York.
**1966** Used almost exclusively for
cruising.
**1973** Registered at Willemstad
under the ownership of NV
Statendam. 24,414 GRT. Cruising
from US ports.

**1** *Passenger and cargo vessel*
Dinteldyk.
**2/3** *The* Statendam *(2), which entered
service in 1957. In (3) she is shown as a
cruise liner with a blue hull and her
new Holland-America Line funnel
markings.*

1

2

3

Turbine steamer *Rotterdam*
Holland-America Line, Rotterdam

Builders: Rotterdamsche DD Mij
Yard no: 300
38,645 GRT; 227.9 × 28.7 m /
748 × 94.1 ft; Parsons geared
turbines, De Schelde; Twin screw;
38,500 SHP; 20.5, max over 22 kn;
Passengers: 655 1st class, 801
tourist class; Crew: 776.

**1958** Sep 13: Launched.
**1959** Jul 12: First trials.
Sep 3: Maiden voyage Rotterdam-
New York.
**1968** 37,783 GRT.
**1969** Used only for cruising.
**1973** Registered at Willemstad
under the ownership of NV
Rotterdam.

**4** *The* Rotterdam, *flagship of the
Holland-America Line. She was the
first sizeable passenger ship to have
large exhaust pipes instead of the
traditional funnels.*

4

Turbine steamer *Ausonia*
'Adriatica' SAN, Venice

Builders: CR dell'Adriatico,
Monfalcone
Yard no: 1821
11,879 GRT; 159.1 × 21.1 m /
522 × 69.2 ft; Parsons geared
turbines from builders; 22,000
SHP; 21, max 23 kn; Passengers:
185 1st class, 135 2nd class, 252
3rd class; Crew: 215.

**1956** Aug 5: Launched.
**1957** Sep 23: Delivered.
Trieste-Beirut service.
Cruising.

**1** *The* Ausonia, *which operates
between Trieste and Beirut.*

1

# Federico C.

Turbine steamer *Federico C.*
Costa Armatori, Genoa

Builders: Ansaldo, Sestri Ponente
Yard no: 1516
20,416 GRT; 184.7 × 24.0 m /
606 × 78.7 ft; Geared turbines
from builders; Twin screw; 30,000
SHP; 21, max 23 kn; Passengers:
243 1st class, 300 2nd class, 736
3rd class.

**1957** Mar 31: Launched.
**1958** Mar: Completed. Registered
under the ownership of Lloyd
Tirrenico SpA.
Mar 22: Maiden voyage Genoa-
Buenos Aires.
Cruising.

**1968** Passengers: 186 1st class,
1,450 tourist class.

**1** *Turbine steamer* Federico C.

1

Turbine steamer *Santa Rosa*
Grace Line, New York

1976 *Samos Sky*

Builders: Newport News SB & DD
Co
Yard no: 521
15,371 GRT; 177.9 × 25.6 m /
584 × 84.0 ft; Geared turbines,
General Electric; 22,000 SHP; 20
kn; Twin screw; Passengers: 300
1st class; Crew: 246.

**1957** Aug 28: Launched.
**1958** Jun 12: Delivered.
New York-Central America
service.
**1959** Mar 26: The *Santa Rosa*
collided with the US tanker
*Valchem* 22 nautical miles off
Atlantic City, NJ. Both ships were
badly damaged, and there was
one death aboard the tanker. The
forepart of the *Santa Rosa* was
burned out.
**1967** 11,353 GRT.
**1970** The Grace Line
amalgamated with Prudential
Lines to form Prudential-Grace
Lines Inc. The new company was
given the Prudential funnel
markings.
**1971** Jan 22: Laid up at Hampton
Roads.
**1975** To the US Department of
commerce. Remained laid up.
**1976** Sold to Vintero Corp, New
York. Renamed *Samos Sky*.
South America service.

*1/2 The sister ships* Santa Paula *(1)
and* Santa Rosa *(2), built for the New
York-Central America service.*

1

Turbine steamer *Santa Paula*
Grace Line, New York

*1972 Stella Polaris*

Builders: Newport News SB &
DD Co
Yard no: 522
15,366 GRT; 177.9 × 25.6 m /
584 × 84.0 ft; Geared turbines,
General Electric; Twin screw;
22,000 SHP; 20 kn; Passengers:
300 1st class; Crew: 246.

**1958** Jan 9: Launched.
Oct 9: Delivered.
New York-Central America
service.
**1967** 11,353 GRT.
**1970** Amalgamation of Grace and
Prudential to form
Prudential-Grace Lines Inc.

**1971** Jan 16: Laid up at Hampton
Roads.
**1972** Sold to Oceanic Sun Line
Special Shipping Co Inc, Piraeus,
a subsidiary of the Marriott Hotel
group. Renamed *Stella Polaris*.
Dec 11: Arrived at Piraeus.
Laid up.
**1976** To be converted at Perama
into a permanently landlocked
hotel ship at Kuwait City, a joint
venture between Marriott and
four Kuwaiti groups.

2

Turbine steamer *Pendennis Castle*
Union-Castle Line, London

1976 *Ocean Queen*

Builders: Harland & Wolff,
Belfast
Yard no: 1558
28,582 GRT; 232.5 × 25.3 m /
763 × 83.0 ft; Parsons geared
turbines, H & W; Twin screw;
46,000 SHP; 22.5 kn; Passengers:
197 1st class, 473 tourist class.

1957 Dec 10: Named. The
launching had to be postponed
because of a strike.
Dec 24: Launched.
1958 Nov: Completed.

1959 Jan 1: Maiden voyage
Southampton-Durban.
1967 28,453 GRT. 28,442 GRT
in 1972.
1976 Aug: Sold to Ocean Queen
Navigation Corp, Panama.
Renamed *Ocean Queen*.

1 The Pendennis Castle, *which entered service in 1958.*

1

Turbine steamer *Windsor Castle*
Union-Castle Line, London

Builders: Cammell Laird & Co,
Birkenhead
Yard no: 1287
37,640 GRT; 238.7 × 28.2 m /
783' × 93.0 ft; Parsons geared
turbines from builders; Twin
screw; 49,000 SHP; 22.5, max 23.5
kn; Passengers: 191 1st class, 591
tourist class; Crew: 475.

**1959** Jun 23: Launched.
**1960** Jun: Completed.
Aug 18: Maiden voyage
Southampton-Durban.
**1967** 36,123 GRT. 36,277 GRT
in 1972.
**1977** Sep: To be withdrawn from
service.

Turbine steamer *Transvaal Castle*
Union-Castle Line, London

1966 *S.A. Vaal*

Builders: Brown, Clydebank
Yard no: 720
32,697 GRT; 231.7 × 27.5 m /
760 × 90.2 ft; Parsons geared
turbines, Brown; Twin screw;
44,000 SHP; 22.5 kn; Passengers:
728 in one class; Crew: 426.

**1961** Jan 17: Launched.
Dec 16: Delivered.
**1962** Jan 18: Maiden voyage
Southampton-Durban.
**1966** Jan 12: Transferred to
South African Marine Corp.
Renamed *S.A. Vaal*. Continued in
the same service under the British
flag.
**1967** 30,212 GRT.
**1969** Feb: Registered at Cape
Town.
**1977** Oct: To be withdrawn from
service.

*2/3 The last new Union-Castle
passenger ships to come into service
were the* Windsor Castle *(2) and*
Transvaal Castle *of 1960 and 1962
respectively. The latter is shown in (3)
as the* S.A. Vaal.

Turbine steamer *Brasil*
Moore-McCormack Lines, New York

1972 *Volendam*
1975 *Monarch Sun*

Builders: Ingalls, Pascagoula
Yard no: 467
14,984 GRT; 188.2 × 26.2 m /
617 × 86.0 ft; Geared turbines,
General Electric; Twin screw;
35,000 SHP; 21, max 24 kn;
Passengers: 553 1st class; Crew:
401.

**1957** Dec 16: Launched.
**1958** Sep 5: Delivered.
Sep 12: Maiden voyage New
York-Buenos Aires.
**1963** Rebuilt by Bethlehem at
Baltimore. 15,257 GRT.

**1969** Sep 5: Laid up at Baltimore.
**1971** Apr: Sold to
Holland-America Line.
**1972** Aug: Handed over.
Renamed *Volendam*.
Aug 18: Arrived at Bremerhaven.
Rebuilt at the Hapag-Lloyd yard.
Registered under the ownership of
Cruiseship NV, Willemstad.
**1973** Feb: To Rotterdam for
further refitting. 23,395 GRT.
Apr: First cruise.
**1974** Jan 6: Laid up at Hampton
Roads.
**1975** Aug: Chartered for two
years to Monarch Cruise and
renamed *Monarch Sun*. Cruising
in the Caribbean.
**1976** Holland-America Line
bought Monarch Cruise Lines Inc

and put *Monarch Sun* under the
Panama flag. 15,631 GRT.

*1-3 Turbine steamer* Brasil *in 1958* (1),
*after her 1963 rebuilding* (2) *and as the*
Volendam *in 1973* (3).

1

2

3

Turbine steamer *Argentina*
Moore-McCormack Lines, New
York

1972 *Veendam*
1974 *Brasil*
1975 *Veendam*
1976 *Edam*

Builders: Ingalls, Pascagoula
Yard no: 468
14,984 GRT; 188.2 × 26.2 m /
617 × 86.0 ft; Geared turbines,
General Electric; Twin screw;
35,000 SHP; 21, max 23.5 kn;
Passengers: 553 1st class; Crew:
401.

**1958** Mar 12: Launched.

Dec 9: Delivered.
Dec 12: Maiden voyage New York-
Buenos Aires.
**1963** Rebuilt at Baltimore by
Bethlehem Steel. 15,257 GRT.
**1971** Apr: Sold to Holland-
America Line.
**1972** Aug: Handed over.
Renamed *Veendam*.
Sep 8: Arrived at Bremerhaven.
Rebuilt at the Hapag-Lloyd yard.
Registered at Willemstad under
the ownership of Cruiseship NV.
**1973** Mar: To Rotterdam for
further refitting. 23,372 GRT.
Jun 17: Began service as cruise
liner with a voyage from

Rotterdam to New York.
**1974** May 14: Laid up at
Hampton Roads.
Dec 15: Chartered to Agence
Maritime International. Renamed
*Brasil*.
Cruising from Rio de Janeiro.
**1975** Apr: End of charter.
Renamed *Veedam*.
Cruising in the Caribbean.
**1976** Registered at Panama and
renamed *Edam*.

4 *The* Veendam *ex* Argentina.
5 *The* Argentina *entering New York.*

4

# The Randfontein

Motorship *Randfontein*
VNSM, The Hague

1971 *Nieuw Holland*
1974 *Yu Hua*

Builders: Wilton-Fijenoord,
Schiedam
Yard no: 760
13,694 GRT; 178.3 × 21.4 m /
585 × 70.2 ft; MAN diesels from
builders; Twin screw; 15,400
BHP; 18 kn; Passengers: 123 1st
class, 166 tourist class.

**1958** Jun 28: Floated in building
dock.
Nov 24: Named and delivered.
**1959** Jan 6: Maiden voyage in
Hamburg-Lourenço Marques
service.
**1971** Jul: Sold to Koninklijke
Java-China Paketvaart Lijnen,
Amsterdam.
Aug: Renamed *Nieuw Holland*.
Service between Japan and
Australia. 13,568 GRT.
**1974** Sold to the People's
Republic of China, with Canton
as home port.
Renamed *Yu Hua*.
China-Africa service.

1/2 *Built for the Africa service, the*
Randfontein (*1*) *entered the Japan-*
*Australia service in 1971 as the* Nieuw
Holland.

1

2

# The Amazon Class

Motorship *Amazon*
Royal Mail Lines, London

1968 *Akaroa*
1971 *Akarita*

Builders: Harland & Wolff,
Belfast
Yard no: 1594
20,368 GRT; 177.7 × 23.8 m /
583 × 78.1 ft; Burmeister &
Wain diesels, H & W; Twin
screw; 20,000 SHP; 17.5 kn;
Passengers: 107 1st class, 82 cabin
class, 275 3rd class.

**1959** Jul 7: Launched.
Dec: Completed. Registered
under the ownership of the Well-
deck Shipping Co.
**1960** Jan 22: Maiden voyage
London-Buenos Aires.
**1967** 18,565 GRT.
**1968** Mar: Sold to Shaw, Savill &
Albion.
May 28: First voyage
Southampton-Australia-New
Zealand.
**1971** Sold to Uglands Rederi,
Grimstad. Renamed *Akarita*.
Rebuilding at Grimstad as a car
transport commenced by Nymo
MV.
**1972** Apr: To the Viktor Lenac
yards at Rijeka. Rebuilding
completed there.
Oct: Car transport. 10,886 GRT.

**1-3** *The Royal Mail liner* Amazon *(1)
is shown in (2) as the* Akarita *and in
(3) after her reconstruction as a car
transport.*

1

2

3

Motorship *Aragon*
Royal Mail Lines, London

1969 *Aranda*
1971 *Hoegh Traveller*

Builders: Harland & Wolff,
Belfast
Yard no: 1595
20,362 GRT; 177.7 × 23.8 m /
583 × 78.1 ft; Burmeister &
Wain diesels, H & W; Twin
screw; 20,000 BHP; 17.5 kn;
Passengers: 107 1st class, 82 cabin
class, 275 3rd class.

**1959** Oct 20: Launched.
**1960** Apr: Completed.
Apr 29: Maiden voyage
London-Buenos Aires.
**1967** 18,575 GRT.
**1969** Sold to Shaw, Savill &
Albion. Renamed *Aranda*.
Mar 28: First voyage
Southampton-Australia-New
Zealand.
**1971** Sold to Leif Hoegh & Co,
Oslo. Renamed *Hoegh Traveller*.
May 12: Arrived at Rijeka.
Rebuilt as a car transport at the
Viktor Lenac yards.
**1972** In service after
reconstruction. 10,912 GRT.

Motorship *Arlanza*
Royal Mail Lines, London

1969 *Arawa*
1971 *Hoegh Transit*
1972 *Hoegh Trotter*

Builders: Harland & Wolff,
Belfast
Yard no: 1596
20,350 GRT; 177.7 × 23.8 m /
583 × 78.1 ft; Burmeister &
Wain diesels, H & W; Twin
screw; 20,000 BHP; 17.5 kn;
Passengers: 107 1st class, 82 cabin
class, 275 3rd class.

**1960** Apr 13: Launched.
Sep 23: Delivered.
Oct 7: Maiden voyage London-
Buenos Aires.
**1967** 18,595 GRT.
**1969** Sold to Shaw, Savill &
Albion. Renamed *Arawa*.
Feb 28: First voyage
Southampton-Australia-New
Zealand.
**1971** Sold to Leif Hoegh & Co,
Oslo. Renamed *Hoegh Transit*.
Jul 1: Arrived at the Viktor Lenac
yards in Rijeka. Rebuilt as a car
transport.
**1972** Jun: Renamed *Hoegh*

*Trotter*. In service as car
transport. 10,895 GRT.

**4-6** *The* Amazon's *sister ships,* Arago
(*4*) *and* Arlanza (*shown in* (*5*) *as the*
*Shaw Savill liner* Arawa) *were also*
*refitted as car transports.* (6) *shows th*
Hoegh Traveller *ex* Aranda *ex* Aragon

4

# The Nuclear-powered Savannah

Turbine steamer *Savannah*
States Marine Lines Inc,
Savannah

Builders: New York SB Co,
Camden
Yard no: 529
13,599 GRT; 181.5 × 23.8 m /
595 × 78.1 ft; De Laval geared
turbines; Single screw; 22,000
SHP; 21, max 23 kn; Passengers:
60 in one class; Crew: 110.

**1959** Jul 21: Launched.
**1961** Dec: Completed. Ordered
by the Maritime Administration
of the US Department of
Commerce, the *Savannah* was the
world's first commercial vessel to
be propelled by nuclear power. A
Babcock & Wilcox reactor
provided the energy to generate
the steam. Trials lasted until
April 1962.

**1962** May 1: Delivered. The
management was transferred to
States Marine Lines.
Aug 20: Maiden voyage
Yorktown, Va-Savannah, then
used for worldwide demonstration
and experimental voyages.
**1964** The *Savannah* used
principally between the USA and
Mediterranean ports. 15,585
GRT.
**1965** Aug 20: The management of
the ship was taken over by First
Atomic Ship Transport Inc, of
American Export Isbrandtsen
Lines. Continued in US-
Mediterranean service but without
passengers.
**1972** Jan 10: Laid up at
Savannah.

1

**1/2** The Savannah, *the first commercial ship in the world to be propelled by nuclear power.*

# Oriana and Canberra

Turbine steamer *Oriana*
P & O-Orient Lines, London

Builders: Vickers-Armstrongs,
Barrow
Yard no: 1061
41,915 GRT; 245.1 × 29.6 m /
804 × 97.1 ft; Parsons geared
turbines from builders; Twin
screw; 80,000 SHP; 27.5, max
30.64 kn; Passengers: 638 1st
class, 1,496 tourist class;Crew:
903.

**1959** Nov 3: Launched.
**1960** Nov 13: Trials.
Dec 3: Maiden voyage
Southampton-Sydney, then via
Auckland and US West Coast
ports back to Southampton.
**1966** Name of P & O-Orient
Lines restyled to P & O Line.
**1973** Cruising only.

Turbo-electric vessel *Canberra*
P & O-Orient Lines, London

Builders: Harland & Wolff,
Belfast
Yard no: 1621
45,270 GRT; 249.9 × 31.1 m /
820 × 102.0 ft; Turbo-electric
propulsion from British Thomson
Houston; Twin screw; 88,000
SHP; 27, max 29.27 kn;
Passengers: 548 1st class, 1,650
tourist class; Crew: 900.

**1960** Mar 16: Launched.
**1961** May 18: Trials.
Jun 2: Maiden voyage
Southampton-Sydney-Auckland-
Transpacific-Southampton.
**1962** 45,733 GRT. 44,807 GRT
in 1968.
**1966** Name of P & O-Orient
Lines restyled P & O Line.
**1973** Cruising.

2

3

**1-3** *The* Oriana *(2) and* Canberra *(1/3), P & O Line's largest passenger ships.*

# Portuguese Liners

Turbine steamer *Infante dom Henrique*
Cia Colonial, Lisbon

Builders: Cockerill, Hoboken
Yard no: 814
23,306 GRT; 195.5 × 24.5 m /
641 × 80.4 ft; Westinghouse
geared turbines, Cockerill; Twin
screw; 22,000 SHP; 21 kn;
Passengers: 156 1st class, 862
tourist class; Crew: 320.

**1960** Apr 29: Launched.
**1961** Sep: Completed.
Lisbon-Beira service.
**1974** The owners' name changed
to Cia Portuguesa de Transportes
Maritimos, as a result of
amalgamation with Carregadores
Acoreanos and Empresa Insulana.
**1976** Jan 3: Laid up at Lisbon.

Turbine steamer *Principe Perfeito*
Cia Nacional, Lisbon

Builders: Swan, Hunter &
Wigham Richardson, Newcastle
Yard no: 1974
19,393 GRT; 190.5 × 23.9 m /
625 × 78.4 ft; Parsons geared
turbines; Twin screw; 24,600
SHP; 20, max 22 kn; Passengers:
200 1st class, 800 tourist class,
200 troops; Crew: 320.

**1960** Sep 22: Launched.
**1961** May 18/19: Trials.
May 31: Delivered.
Jun 27: Maiden voyage Lisbon-
Beira.
**1976** Apr: Swan Hunter Ship
Repairs began conversion of liner

as an accommodation ship for
dockers. Renamed *Al Hasa*.
Jun 14: Sailed for Damman.

*1/2 Portuguese shipping companies
placed the* Infante Dom Henrique *(1)
and the* Principe Perfeito *(2) in the
Lisbon-Beira service in 1961.*

Turbine steamer *France*
CGT, Le Havre

Builders: Penhoët, St Nazaire
Yard no: G19
66,348 GRT; 315.5 × 33.7 m /
1035 × 110.5 ft; CEM-Parsons
geared turbines from builders;
Quadruple screw; 160,000 SHP;
31, max 35.21 kn; Passengers:
407 1st class, 1,637 tourist class.

**1960** May 11: Launched.
**1961** Nov 19: First trials.
**1962** Jan 19: Cruise Le Havre-

Canary Islands.
Feb 3: Maiden voyage Le Havre-
New York.
Cruising.
**1974** Jul: After the French
government announced that it was
not prepared to pay any more
subsidies for the *France*, CGT
made it known that they would
withdraw their flagship from
service on October 25 1974.
Sep: Just as the ship was about to
berth at Le Havre French trade
unionists took over from the

officers and anchored the ship in
the fairway. This was a protest
against the threatened loss of their
jobs. The passengers were
disembarked by tender.
Oct 9: After the strikers'
enthusiasm had diminished, the
*France* was berthed and was later
laid up at Le Havre.

1 *TS* France, *since 1972 the largest
passenger ship in the world.*

1

Turbine steamer *Galileo Galilei*
Lloyd Triestino, Genoa

Builders: CR dell'Adriatico,
Monfalcone
Yard no: 1862
27,888 GRT; 213.9 × 28.6 m /
702 × 93.8 ft; De Laval geared
turbines from builders; Twin
screw; 44,000 SHP; 24, max 26.4
kn; Passengers: 156 1st class,
1,594 tourist class; Crew: 443.

**1961** Jul 2: Launched.
**1963** Mar: Completed.
Apr 22: Maiden voyage Genoa-
Sydney.
**1964** 27,907 GRT.

Turbine steamer *Guglielmo
Marconi*
Lloyd Triestino, Genoa

Builders: CR dell'Adriatico,
Monfalcone
Yard no: 1863
27,905 GRT; 213.9 × 28.6 m /
902 × 93.8 ft; De Laval geared
turbines from builders; Twin
screw; 44,000 SHP; 24, max over
26 kn; Passengers: 156 1st class,
1,594 tourist class; Crew: 443.

**1961** Sep 24: Launched.
**1963** Oct: Completed.
Nov 18: Maiden voyage Genoa-
Sydney.
**1976** Jan: Naples-La Plata service.

*1/2 The* Guglielmo Marconi (*1*) *and*
Galileo Galilei *went into service
between Genoa and Sydney, where the
latter is illustrated* (*2*).

1

**The Ru Yung**

Motorship *Ru Yung*
Chinese Maritime Trust Ltd,
Keelung

Builders: Uraga Dock Co,
Yokosuka
Yard no: 798
10,343 GRT; 158.0 × 20.2 m /
518 × 66.3 ft; Sulzer diesels from
builders; Single screw; 12,000
BHP; 18 kn; Passengers: 14 1st
class, 12 tourist class.

**1961** Oct 10: Launched.
Dec 25: Delivered.
Formosa-USA service.

1 *The* Ru Yung *of the Chinese
Maritime Trust was fitted with
accommodation for 26 passengers.*

Motorship *Anna Nery*
Cia Nacional de Nav Costeira
Autarquia Federal, Rio de Janeiro

Builders: 'Uljanik', Pula
Yard no: 237
10,444 GRT; 150.0 × 19.0 m /
492 × 62.3 ft; Krupp-Burmeister
& Wain diesels from builders;
Twin screw; 9,100 BHP; 16, max
19.1 kn; Passengers: 208 1st class,
274 tourist class; Crew: 163.

**1961** Nov 5: Launched.
**1962** Aug 27: Delivered.
Manáus-Buenos Aires service.
**1963** Oct 13: During a voyage
from Haifa to Buenos Aires the
*Anna Nery* collided with the
Brazilian tanker *Presidente
Deodoro* 25 nautical miles off
Rio de Janeiro. The liner was
badly damaged and had to be
towed into Rio. The accident
claimed two lives. After a month of
repair work she resumed service.

**1968** Sold to Lloyd Brasileiro.
**1972** 12,433 GRT.

Motorship *Rosa da Fonseca*
Cia Nacional de Nav Costeira
Autarquia Federal, Rio de Janeiro

**1975** *P/S Seven Seas*

Builders: 'Split' Brodogradiliste,
Split
Yard no: 169
10,444 GRT; 150.0 × 19.0 m /
492 × 62.3 ft; Krupp-Burmeister
& Wain diesels from builders;
Twin screw; 9,100 BHP; 16, max
19 kn; Passengers: 208 1st class,
274 tourist class; Crew: 163.

**1961** Dec 29: Launched.
**1962** Oct 28: Delivered.
Manáus-Buenos Aires service.
**1968** Sold to Lloyd Brasileiro.
**1972** 12,433 GRT.
**1975** To Cosmos Passenger
Service, Panama. Renamed *P/S
Seven Seas*. Chartered to Mitsui-
OSK Lines for four years.
Aug 6: First cruise Yokohama-
Hawaii.

*1/2 The* Anna Nery, *shown in (1) in
Lloyd Brasileiro colours, and the* Rosa
de Fonseca, *were built for the South
American coastal service.*

1

2

Turbine steamer *Santa Magdalena*
Grace Line, New York

Builders: Bethlehem SB Corp,
Sparrow's Point
Yard no: 4585
14,443 GRT; 166.7 × 24.1 m /
547 × 79.0 ft; Geared turbines,
General Electric; Single screw;
19,800 SHP; 20 kn; Passengers:
127 1st class; Crew: 128.

**1962** Feb 13: Launched.
**1963** Feb 4: Delivered.
Feb 15: Maiden voyage New York-
Central America.
**1967** 11,219 GRT.
**1970** Grace and Prudential
amalgamated to form Prudential-
Grace Lines.
**1972** North America West Coast-
Panama Canal-Buenos Aires-
Valparaiso service.

Turbine steamer *Santa Mariana*
Grace Line, New York

Builders: Bethlehem SB Corp,
Sparrow's Point
Yard no: 4586
14,442 GRT; 166.7 × 24.1 m /
547 × 79.0 ft; Geared turbines,
General Electric; Single screw;
19,800 SHP; 20 kn; Passengers:
127 1st class; Crew: 128.

**1962** May 11: Launched.
**1963** Jun 14: Delivered.
New York-Central America
service.
**1967** 11,188 GRT.
**1970** Grace and Prudential
amalgamated to form Prudential-
Grace Lines Inc.
**1972** North America West Coast-
Panama Canal-Buenos Aires-
Valparaiso service.

*1/2 The combined passenger and
container vessels* Santa Magdalena *(1)
and* Santa Mariana *(2), which entered
service in 1963/64.*
*3 The* Santa Mariana *with the funnel
with which all ships of the class were
fitted in 1967.*

1

2

3

Turbine steamer *Santa Maria*
Grace Line, New York

Builders: Bethlehem SB Corp,
Sparrow's Point
Yard no: 4587
14,442 GRT; 166.7 × 24.1 m /
547 × 79.0 ft; Geared turbines,
General Electric; Single screw;
19,800 SHP; 20 kn; Passengers:
127 1st class; Crew: 128.

**1962** Oct 9: Launched.
**1963** Sep 23: Delivered.
New York-Central America
service.
**1967** 11,188 GRT.
**1970** Grace and Prudential
amalgamated to form Prudential-
Grace Lines, Inc.
**1972** North America West Coast-
Panama Canal-Buenos Aires-
Valparaiso service.

Turbine steamer *Santa Mercedes*
Grace Line, New York

Builders: Bethlehem SB Corp,
Sparrow's Point
Yard no: 4602
14,442 GRT; 166.7 × 24.1 m /
547 × 79.0 ft; Geared turbines,
General Electric; Single screw;
19,800 SHP; 20 kn; Passengers:
127 1st class; Crew: 128.

**1963** Jul 30: Launched.
**1964** Apr 7: Delivered.
New York-Central America
service.
**1967** 11,188 GRT.
**1970** Grace and Prudential
amalgamated to form
Prudential-Grace Lines Inc.
**1972** North America West Coast-
Panama Canal-Buenos Aires-
Valparaiso service.

**4/5** *The* Santa Maria (*3*) *and* Santa
Mercedes (*4*).

# Ancerville and Renaissance

Motorship *Ancerville*
Cie de Nav Paquet, Marseille

1973 *Minghua*

Builders: Penhoët, St Nazaire
Yard no: M21
14,225 GRT; 167.5 × 21.8 m /
549 × 71.5 ft; Burmeister &
Wain diesels from builders; Twin
screw; 26,700 BHP; 22.5 kn;
Passengers: 171 1st class, 346
tourist class, 253 3rd class; Crew:
173.

**1962** Apr 5: Launched.
Aug 20: Delivered.
Sep 5: First voyage, a cruise to the
Canary Islands.
Marseille-Dakar service.
**1970** To Nouvelle Cie de
Paquebots.
**1973** Apr: Sold to the People's
Republic of China. Renamed
*Minghua*.
Service between China and East
Africa of the China Ocean
Shipping Co.

Motorship *Renaissance*
Cie Francaise de Nav, Marseille

Builders: Penhoët, St Nazaire
yard no: D23
11,724 GRT; 150.0 × 21.0 m /
492 × 68.9 ft; Burmeister &
Wain diesels from builders; Twin
screw; 13,600 BHP; 18.5, max 20
kn; Passengers: 416 in one class;
Crew: 191.

**1965** Dec 11: Launched.
**1966** May 10: Delivered.
Marseille-Haifa service.
Cruising.
**1970** Sold to Nouvelle Cie de
Paquebots.

1/2 *The* Ancerville (*1*) *was sold to the People's Republic of China in 1973 and renamed* Minghua.
3 *The* Renaissance, *used mainly for cruising.*

1

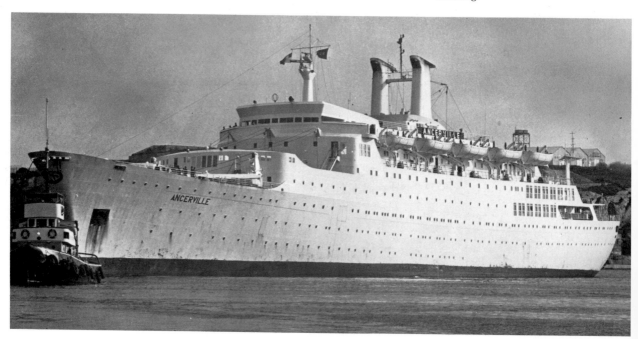

2

3

**Michelangelo and Raffaello**

Turbine steamer *Michelangelo*
'Italia' SAN, Genoa

Builders: Ansaldo, Sestri Ponente
Yard no: 1577
45,911 GRT; 276.2 × 30.1 m /
906 × 98.7 ft; Geared turbines
from builders; Twin screw; 87,000
SHP; 26.5, max 29 kn;
Passengers: 535 1st class, 550
cabin class, 690 tourist class;
Crew: 720.

**1962** Sep 16: Launched.
**1965** Apr: Completed.
May 12: Maiden voyage Genoa-
New York.
**1966** Apr 12: In a fierce Atlantic
storm the *Michelangelo* was badly
damaged when heavy seas broke
aboard. Two passengers and one
crew member were killed.
**1974** Used mainly for cruising.
**1975** Jul 5: Laid up at Genoa.
**1976** Sep 15: Laid up at La
Spezia.
Dec: Sold to Government of Iran
for use as an accommodation
ship.

Turbine steamer *Raffaello*
'Italia' SAN, Genoa

Builders: CR dell'Adriatico,
Trieste
Yard no: 1864
45,933 GRT; 275.5 × 30.2 m /
904 × 99.1 ft; Geared turbines,
Ansaldo; Twin screw; 87,000
SHP; 26.5, max 30.5 kn;
Passengers: 535 1st class, 550
cabin class, 690 tourist class;
Crew: 720.

**1963** Mar 24: Launched.
**1965** Jul: Completed.
Jul 10: First voyage,
Mediterranean cruise.
Jul 25: Maiden voyage Genoa-
New York.
**1965** Oct 31: After a fire in the
engine room the *Raffaello* had to
limp back to Genoa on one
propeller.
**1974** Mainly cruising.
**1975** Apr 21: Last voyage from
New York.
Jun 6: Laid up at La Spezia.
**1976** Dec: Sold to Government of
Iran for use as accommodation
ship.

**1-3** *From 1974 'Italia' also began a
drastic reduction in its North Atlantic
service and used the sister ships*
Michelangelo *(1) and* Raffaello *(2)
mainly for cruising. (3) shows the two
ships at Genoa, the* Raffaello *on the
left.*

1

Motorship *Sakura Maru*
Nihon Sangyo Junko Mihonichi
Kyokai, Tokyo

1971 *Sakura*

Builders: Mitsubishi, Kobe
Yard no: 933
12,628 GRT; 157.0 × 21.0 m /
515 × 68.9 ft; Sulzer diesels from
builders; Single screw; 9,800 BHP;
17.5 kn; Passengers: 152 1st class,
800 tourist class.

**1962** Jun 22: Launched.
Oct 15: Delivered.
Nov 5: Maiden voyage Kobe-
Jeddah. The *Sakura Maru* served
as an exhibition ship for Japanese
industrial products. When she was
not so engaged, she sailed in the
Yokohama-America passenger
service, managed by Mitsui-OSK
Lines.

**1970** 12,470 GRT.
**1971** Sold to Mitsubishi Shintaku
Ginko KK, Tokyo. Renamed
*Sakura*.
Dec: First voyage Tokyo-Okinawa
for Oshima Unyu KK,
Kagoshima.
**1973** Jun: Cruising from Tokyo.

*1/2 The* Sakura Maru *(1) and* Shin
Sakura Maru *(2) voyaged round the
world as exhibition ships promoting
Japanese industrial goods.
3 The* Sakura *in September 1973.*

Motorship *Shin Sakura Maru*
Nihon Sangyo Junko Mihonichi
Kyokai, Tokyo

Builders: Mitsubishi, Kobe
Yard no: 1033
13,082 GRT; 175.8 × 24.6 m /
577 × 80.7 ft; Diesels from
builders; Single screw; 21,600
BHP; 20.5 kn; Passengers: 92 1st
class.

**1971** Dec 18: Launched.
**1972** Jul 18: Delivered.
Jul 27: Maiden voyage
Tokyo-Europe as floating fair to
promote Japanese industrial
products.
When not so engaged, the *Shin
Sakura Maru* is used in the
Mitsui-OSK Lines' Japan-America
service, also on other routes. No
passengers carried since 1973.

1

2

3

# Zim Israel Liner Shalom

Turbine steamer *Shalom*
Zim Israel Navigation Co, Haifa

1967 *Hanseatic*
1973 *Doric*

Builders: Penhoët, St Nazaire
Yard no: Z21
25,338 GRT; 191.7 × 24.8 m /
629 × 81.3 ft; Parsons geared
turbines from builders; Twin
screw; 25,000 SHP; 20, max 22.7
kn; Passengers: 72 1st class, 1,018
tourist class; Crew: 469.

**1962** Nov 10: Launched. The
names *King Salomon* and *King
David* had originally been
considered.

**1964** Mar 3: Completed.
Apr 17: Maiden voyage Haifa-
New York.
Oct: Passenger accommodation
refitted by Wilton -Fijenoord. 148
1st class, 864 tourist class.
Nov 26: The *Shalom* collided with
the Norwegian tanker *Stolt Dagali*
off New York. The tanker broke
in two and sank.
**1967** May: Sold to German
Atlantic Line, Hamburg.
Nov 9: Handed over. Renamed
*Hanseatic*. 23,320 GRT.
Dec 16: The *Hanseatic's* first
voyage under the German flag was
a private cruise. Then used for

Hamburg-New York service and
cruising.
**1969** Cruising only.
**1973** Jul: Sold to Home Lines,
Panama.
Sep 25: Handed over at Genoa.
Renamed *Doric*. Used by Home
Lines for cruising.
**1976** 17,884 GRT.

1/2 *The flagship of the Israeli
merchant fleet, the* Shalom *(1), was
sold to Germany to become the*
Hanseatic *(2) in 1967.*

1

Turbine steamer *Oceanic*
Home Lines, Panama

Builders: CR dell'Adriatico,
Monfalcone
Yard no: 1876
27,644 GRT; 238.5 × 29.4 m /
782 × 96.4 ft; De Laval geared
turbines from builders; Twin
screw; 60,500 SHP; 26.6 max
27.25 kn; Passengers: 1,200 in one
class; Crew: 560.

**1963** Jan 15: Launched.
**1965** Mar 31: Delivered.
Apr 3: Maiden voyage Genoa-New
York.
Apr 24: First voyage New York-
Bahamas.
Originally intended for Cuxhaven-
Montreal service, the *Oceanic* was
used primarily for cruising from
New York.

1 *The* Oceanic, *Home Lines' largest
and only ship built for the company.*

1

# The Ivan Franko Class

Motorship *Ivan Franko*
USSR, Odessa (Black Sea
Steamship Co)

Builders: Mathias-Thesen yard,
Wismar
19,861 GRT; 176.1 × 23.6 m /
578 × 77.4 ft; Sulzer diesels, De
Scheldé; Twin screw; 21,000 BHP;
20 kn; Passengers: 750 in one
class; Crew: 220.

**1963** Jun 15: Launched.
**1964** Nov 14: Delivered.
Cruising and Leningrad-Montreal
service.
**1974** 20,064 GRT.
**1975** Cruising only.

Motorship *Aleksandr Pushkin*
USSR, Leningrad (Baltic
Steamship Co)

Builders: Mathias-Thesen yard,
Wismar
19,860 GRT; 176.1 × 23.6 m /
578 × 77.4 ft; MAN diesels,
Dieselmot works, Rostock; Twin
screw; 21,000 BHP; 20 kn;
Passengers: 750 in one class;
Crew: 220.

**1964** Mar 26: Launched.
**1965** Jun: Completed.
Cruising.
**1966** Apr 13: First voyage
Leningrad-Montreal.
**1975** Cruising only. 20,502 GRT.

Motorship *Taras Shevchenko*
USSR, Odessa (Black Sea
Steamship Co)

Builders: Mathias-Thesen yard,
Wismar
19,549 GRT; 176.1 × 23.6 m /
578 × 77.4 ft; Sulzer diesels,
Cegielski; Twin screw; 21,000
BHP; 20 kn; Passengers: 750 in
one class; Crew: 220.

**1965** Jan 16: Launched.
**1967** Apr 26: Delivered.
Cruising.
**1975** 20,027 GRT.

**1-3** *Between 1964 and 1972 the Soviet
State shipping company placed five
ships in service that had been built at
Wismar.* Ivan Franko *(1),* Aleksandr
Pushkin *(2) and* Taras Shevshenko *(3).*

1

Motorship *Shota Rustaveli*
USSR, Odessa (Black Sea
Steamship Co)

Builders: Mathias-Thesen yard,
Wismar
19,567 GRT; 176.1 × 23.6 m /
578 × 77.4 ft; Sulzer diesels,
Cegielski; Twin screw; 21,000
BHP; 20 kn; Passengers: 750 in
one class; Crew: 220.

**1967** Launched.
**1968** May: Completed.
Jun 30: Delivered.
Cruising.
**1975** 20,146 GRT.

Motorship *Mikhail Lermontov*
USSR, Leningrad (Baltic
Steamship Co)

Builders: Mathias-Thesen yard,
Wismar
Yard no: 129
19,872 GRT; 176.0 × 23.6 m /
577 × 77.4 ft; Sulzer diesels,
Cegielski; Twin screw; 21,000
BHP; 20 kn; Passengers: 700 in
one class; Crew: 300.

**1970** Dec 31: Launched.
**1972** Feb: Completed.
Apr 21: Maiden cruise
Bremerhaven-Canary Islands.

Jun 9: First voyage Bremerhaven-
Montreal.
**1973** May 28: First voyage
Leningrad-New York. The
*Mikhail Lermontov* was the first
Soviet passenger ship to sail in
Transatlantic service to New
York.
North Atlantic service
June-August, besides cruising.
**1975** Cruising only.

**4/5** Shota Rustaveli (*4*) *and* Mikhail
Lermontov (*5*), *the last two ships of the
class.*

4

5

Motorship *Empress of Australia*
Australian Coastal Shipping
Commission, Hobart

Builders: Cockatoo D & E Co,
Sydney
Yard no: 220
12,037 GRT; 135.6 × 21.5 m /
445 × 70.5 ft; MAN diesels; Twin
screw; 13,500 BHP; 18.5, max
21.5 kn; Passengers: 250 in one
class; Crew: 106; Vehicles: 91
cars, 16 lorries.

**1964** Jan 18: Launched.
**1965** Jan: Completed.
Used in Australian coastal service
Sydney-Hobart-Bell Bay-Burnie.
**1973** 8,196 GRT.

1 *The* Empress of Australia *was built
for the Australian coastal service.*

1

# Norwegian America Liners

Motorship *Sagafjord*
Norwegian America Line, Oslo

Builders: F et Ch de la
Méditerranée, La Seyne
Yard no: 1366
24,002 GRT; 189.0 × 24.9 m /
620 × 81.7 ft; Sulzer diesels from
builders; Twin screw; 27,000
BHP; 20, max 22.5 kn;
Passengers: 85 1st class, 704
tourist class; 462 passengers in
one class when cruising; Crew:
350.

**1964** Jun 13: Launched.
**1965** May: First trials.
Sep 18: Delivered.
Oct 2: Maiden voyage Oslo-
New York.
Used mainly for cruising.
The shipyard went into
liquidation in 1966 because of the
losses incurred through the
building of this ship.

Motorship *Vistafjord*
Norwegian America Line, Oslo

Builders: Swan Hunter Group;
Wallsend
24,292 GRT; 191.1 × 24.4 m /
627 × 80.0 ft; Sulzer diesels,
Clark; Twin screw; 32,000 BHP;
20, max over 23 kn; Passengers:
550-620 in one class; Crew: 390.

**1972** May 15: Launched.
**1973** Apr 6: Trials.
May 15: Delivered.
May 22: Maiden voyage Oslo-
New York.
Used for worldwide cruising.

**1/2** *The latest Norwegian America
Line passenger ships,* Sagafjord (*1*)
*and* Vistafjord (*2*).

1

2

**Costa Liner Eugenio C.**

Turbine steamer *Eugenio C.*
Costa Armatori, Genoa

Builders: CR dell'Adriatico,
Monfalcone
Yard no: 1884
30,567 GRT; 217.4 × 29.3 m /
713 × 96.1 ft; De Laval geared
turbines from builders; Twin
screw; 60,500 SHP; 27, max 28.4
kn; passengers: 178 1st class, 356
2nd class, 1,102 tourist class;
Crew: 424.

**1964** Nov 21: Launched.
**1966** Aug 22: Delivered.
Genoa-Buenos Aires service.
Cruising.

*1/2 The* Eugenio C. *in Hamburg
harbour in 1967.*

Motorship *Kungsholm*
Swedish-America Line,
Gothenburg

Builders: Brown, Clydebank
Yard no: 728
26,678 GRT; 201.2 × 26.3 m /
660 × 86.3 ft; Götaverken
diesels; Twin screw; 27,700 BHP;
21, max 23 kn; Passengers: 108
1st class, 605 tourist class; 450
pasengers in one class when
cruising; Crew: 438.

**1965** Apr 14: Launched.
**1965** Nov 19: First trials.
**1966** Mar 17: Delivered.
Apr 22: Maiden voyage
Gothenburg-New York.
Used mainly for cruising.
**1975** Aug: Sold to Flagship
Cruises, Monrovia.
Oct 6: Handed over.
Cruising from New York.
**1976** 18,174 GRT.

1 *The* Kungsholm, *which entered service in 1966.*

1

Motorship *Italia*
Sunsarda SpA, Trieste

Builders: CN Felszegi, Trigoso
Yard no: 76
12,219 GRT; 150.0 × 20.7 m /
492 × 67.9 ft; Sulzer diesels,
Adriatico, Twin screw; 16,400
BHP; 19, max 21 kn; Passengers:
500 in one class.

**1965** Apr 28: Launched.
**1967** Aug: Delivered.
Cruising.
Sold to Crociere d'Oltremare,
Cagliari. Used for
Acapulco-Seattle service and for
cruising in North American
waters.
**1974** Oct: Sold to Costa
Armatori, Genoa.

Continued cruising in North and
Central American waters.

**1** *The motorship* Italia.

Motorship *Pasteur*
Messageries Maritimes, Dunkirk

1973 *Chidambaram*

Builders: A et Ch de Dunquerque et Bordeaux, Dunkirk
Yard no: 247
17,986 GRT; 174.0 × 24.0 m / 571 × 78.7 ft; Sulzer diesels; Twin screw; 24,000 BHP; 20, max 24 kn; Passengers: 163 1st class, 266 tourist class.

**1966** Jun 2: Launched. The ship had been ordered in 1963 as the *Australien* for the Messageries Maritime Australia service. Renamed before launching.
Oct 27: Delivered.
Hamburg-Buenos Aires service.
**1972** Oct: Sold to The Shipping Corporation of India Ltd, Bombay. Rebuilt by Amsterdam DD Mij.

**1973** Mar: Renamed *Chidambaram*. 17,226 GRT. 154 passengers in cabins, 1,526 in dormitories.
Apr: First voyage in India-Singapore service.

*1/2 The* Pasteur *(1) was sold to Indian owners in 1972 and renamed* Chidambaram *in the following year.*

1

2

**Pakistani Passenger Ships**

Motorship *Ocean Endurance*
Trans Oceanic SS Co Ltd,
Karachi

Builders: Bartram & Sons,
Sunderland
Yard no: 407
10,308 GRT; 153.3 × 20.2 m /
503 × 66.3 ft; Sulzer diesels,
Hawthorn; Single screw; 9,600
BHP; 17 kn; Passengers: 26 1st
class, 250 3rd class; Crew: 90.

**1966** Jun 20: Launched.
Dec: Completed.
Karachi-Chittagong service.
7,795 GRT as shelter decker.
**1971** Used on various routes
following the Indo-Pakistani war.

Motorship *Ohrmazd*
East & West SS Co, Karachi

Builders: Burntisland SB Co
Yard no: 418
11,046 GRT; 158.6 × 20.4 m /
520 × 66.9 ft; Sulzer diesels,
Clark; Single screw; 10,000 BHP;
19 kn; Passengers: 26 1st class,
250 3rd class; Crew: 88.

**1967** Apr 25: Launched.
**1968** Completed.
Karachi-Chittagong service. 7,963
GRT as shelter decker.
**1971** Used on various routes
following the Indo-Pakistani war.

1

1/2 *The motorships* Ocean Edurance
*and* Ohrmazd *were built for the
Karachi-Chittagong service.*

Motorship *Heleanna*
C.S. Efthymiadis, Piraeus

Ex *Munkedal*

Builders: Götaverken,
Gothenburg
Yard no: 679
11,674 GRT; 167.3 × 20.2 m /
549 × 66.3 ft; Diesels from
builders; Single screw; 6,750
BHP; 15 kn; Passengers: 620 in
one class; Crew: 94; 220 vehicles.

**1953** Nov 10: Launched as tanker
*Munkedal*.
**1954** Jan 21: Completed. Tanker
service for Munkedals A/B.
11,232 GRT.
**1966** Bought by C.S.
Efthymiadis. Renamed *Heleanna*.
Rebuilt at Piraeus as passenger
and car ferry.
**1967** Car ferry service between
Patras and Ancona.
**1971** Aug 28: During a voyage
from Patras to Ancona the
*Heleanna* caught fire off Brindisi.
The fire, which had started in the
early morning through an
electrical fault in the galley, soon
spread. With 1,128 people on
board she was extremely
overcrowded and panic broke
out. Crew and passengers
abandoned the burning *Heleanna*
in disorder. 26 people died. The
survivors were picked up by
fishing boats and other vessels
called to the scene.
**1974** Feb: The wreck of the
*Heleanna* was sold to be broken
up at La Spezia and arrived at the
Diana Lotti breakers' yard on
February 16.
Resold and converted to a dumb
lighter at Toulon.

Motorship *Kydon*
Cretan Maritime Co SA, Canea

Ex *Wirakel*

Builders: P. Smit, Rotterdam
Yard no: 605
10,714 GRT; 154.0 × 20.0 m /
505 × 65.6 ft; Diesels from
builders; Single screw; 5,530
BHP; 14.5 kn; Passengers: 860 in
one class.

**1953** Mar 28: Launched as tanker
*Wirakel* for Phs van Ommeren
NV.
Jun: Completed for Suomen
Tankkilaiva O/Y, Helsinki.
9,583, later 10,016 GRT.
**1968** Bought by Cretan Maritime
Co. Renamed *Kydon*. Rebuilt as a
car and passenger ferry.
**1970** Car ferry between Piraeus
and Khania (Crete).

*1/2 The car ferries* Heleanna *(1) and* Kydon *(2) were originally built as tankers.*

# The Amelia de Mello

Turbine steamer *Amelia de Mello*
Soc Geral de Commercio, Lisbon

Ex *Zion*
1972 *Ithaca*

Builders: Deutsche Werft,
Hamburg
Yard no: 691
10,195 GRT; 152.7 × 19.8 m /
501 × 64.9 ft; AEG geared
turbines; Single screw; 10,500
SHP; 19 kn; Passengers: 355 in
two classes.

**1955** Jul 19: Launched as *Zion* for
Zim Israel Line, Haifa.
**1956** Feb 12: Delivered. 9,831
GRT.
Feb 19: First voyage Hamburg-
Haifa.
Mar 9: Maiden voyage Haifa-New
York.
**1966** Sold to Soc Geral de
Commercio, Lisbon.
Renamed *Amelia de Mello*.
10,195 GRT. Lisbon-Canary
Islands service.
**1971** Aug 7: Laid up at Lisbon.

**1972** Sold to Cia de Vapores
Realma SA, Piraeus.
Renamed *Ithaca*.
May 9: Arrived at Bilbao and
there rebuilt for cruising. 780
passengers in one class.
**1973** May: Placed in service.
Cruising in the Mediterranean.
8,977 GRT.

*1/2 In 1966 the Soc Geral de
Commercio bought the Israeli* Zion,
*then the 10,195 GRT* Amelia de Mello
*(1). (2) shows the latter in 1973 as the*
Ithaca.

1

2

Motorship *Yaohua*
People's Republic of China,
Canton
China National Ocean Shipping
Co)

Builders: Penhoët, St Nazaire
Yard no: N23
10,151 GRT; 148.8 × 21.0 m /
488 × 68.9 ft; Sulzer diesels,
Constr Méc; Twin screw; 15,000
BHP; 21.5 kn; Passengers: 100 1st
class, 100 2nd class, 188 3rd class;
Crew: 177.

**1966** Dec 10: Launched.
**1967** Aug 20: Delivered.
China-East Africa service.

**1** *The first purpose-built passenger ship for the People's Republic of China, the* Yaohua.

1

Turbine steamer *Queen Elizabeth 2*
Cunard Line, Southampton

Builders: Brown, Clydebank
Yard no: 736
65,863 GRT; 293.5 × 32.0 m / 963 × 105.0 ft; Geared turbines from builders: Twin screw; 110,000 SHP; 28.5, max 32.46 kn; passengers: 564 1st class, 1,441 tourist class, 1,400 in one class when cruising; Crew: 906.

**1967** Sep 20: Launched.
**1968** Nov 26-29: First trials.
Dec 17-19: Second trials.
Dec 23: Maiden voyage from Greenock to the Canary Islands. On the way a fault developed in the turbines, forcing the ship to return to her builders. As the passenger accommodation also had not been completed, Cunard refused to accept the ship on the planned date of January 1 1969.
**1969** Apr 1-8: Renewed trials.
Apr 18: Delivered.
May 2: Maiden voyage Southampton-New York.
Used mainly for cruising.
**1971** Jan 9: Took part in rescuing passengers and crew of the burning French liner *Antilles* in Caribbean waters.
**1972** Passenger accommodation altered. 604 1st class, 1,223 tourist class, 1,740 in one class when cruising.
**1974** Apr 1: 270 nautical miles southwest of the Bermudas the boilers were put out of action as a result of a damaged fuel pipe. The ship drifted in the Atlantic, devoid of power. After a provisional repair done with materials available on board had held for only 30 minutes, the 1,654 passengers were transferred at sea on April 3 to the Norwegian cruise liner *Sea Venture*.
Apr 5: The *Queen Elizabeth 2* was towed into Hamilton on April 7 by the tugs *Joan Moran* and *Elizabeth Moran* and underwent repairs.
**1976** Jul 23: Engine room fire off the Scilly Islands caused serious damage to starboard engine. Put back to Southampton, repaired, completed trials and sailed.

*1/2 The British superliner* Queen Elizabeth 2.

1

2

# The Hamburg

Turbine steamer *Hamburg*
German Atlantic Line, Hamburg

1973 *Hanseatic*
1974 *Maksim Gorkij*

Builders: Deutsche Werft,
Hamburg
Yard no: 825
25,022 GRT; 194.7 × 26.6 m /
639 × 87.2 ft; AEG geared
turbines; Twin screw; 23,000
SHP; 20, max 23.5 kn;
Passengers: 652 in one class;
Crew: 403.

**1968** Feb 21: Launched.
**1969** Feb 12-15: Trials.
Mar 20: Delivered.
Mar 28: Maiden cruise Cuxhaven-
South America.
**1973** 24,981 GRT.
Sep 25: Renamed *Hanseatic*.
Dec 1: The German Atlantic Line
ran into financial difficulites and
ceased operations. The *Hanseatic*
was laid up at Hamburg.
Dec 12: After a sale to the
Japanese Ryutsu Kaiun KK failed
to materialise, the liner was sold

to the Robin International Corp,
New York, which acquired the
ship on behalf of the Soviet state
shipping company.
**1974** Jan 25: Handed over to the
Black Sea SS Co, Odessa.
Renamed *Maksim Gorkij*.
Worldwide cruising.

**1/2** *In December 1973 the German
Atlantic Line sold its last passenger
ship, the* Hanseatic *ex* Hamburg *(1) to
the Soviet Union, which in 1974 placed
her in service as the* Maksim Gorkij.
*(2).*

1

2

Motorship *Freeport I*
Freeport Cruise Liners Inc,
Monrovia

Launched as *Freeport*
1973 *Freeport*
1974 *Svea Star*
1976 *Caribe*

Builders: LMG Lübeck
Yard no: 658
10,488 GRT; 134.4 × 21.5 m /
441 × 70.5 ft; OEW Pielstick
geared diesels; Twin screw; 16,000
BHP; 20, max 21.4 kn;
Passengers: 812 in one class; Car
deck for 144 cars.

**1968** Apr 20: Launched as
*Freeport*.
Nov 16: Trials.
Nov 22: Delivered. Renamed

*Freeport I.*
Used for cruising from Miami and
for the Miami-Freeport service.
**1973** Sold to the Birka Line A/B,
Mariehamm. Renamed *Freeport*.
9,963 GRT.
Oct: Resold to Stockholm Rederi
A/B Svea, Stockholm.
**1974** Renamed *Svea Star*.
Mar: First voyage Helsingborg-
Travemünde.
**1976** Mar: Sold to Bremer
Schiffahrts-Gesellschaft mbH &
Co KG, Bremen for delivery in
October.
Nov 4: Renamed *Caribe*.
Cruising in Caribbean.

**1** *The motorship* Freeport I.

1

**Motorship *Starward***
Klosters Rederi A/S, Oslo

Builders: AG 'Weser', Seebeck
yard, Bremerhaven
Yard no: 935
12,949 GRT; 160.1 × 22.8 m /
525 × 74.8 ft; MAN diesels; Twin
screw; 17,380 BHP; 21.5 kn;
Passengers: 736 in one class;
Crew: 225.

**1968** Apr 27: The 90 m (295 ft)
long after section was launched;
forepart built in dry dock.
Jun 21: Floated in building dock.
Nov 29: Delivered.
Dec 21: First cruise from Miami.
Seven-day cruises in the
Caribbean.

**Motorship *Skyward***
Klosters Rederi A/S, Oslo

Builders: AG 'Weser', Seebeck
yard, Bremerhaven
Yard no: 942
16,254 GRT; 160.1 × 22.8 m /
525 × 74.8 ft; MAN diesels; Twin
screw; 17,380 BHP; 21.3 kn;
Passengers: 930 in one class;
Crew: 250.

**1969** Apr 27: The 90 m (295 ft)
long after section was launched;
forepart built in dry dock.
Jun 28: Floated in building dock.
Dec 10: Delivered.
14-day cruises from Miami in the
Caribbean.

**Motorship *Southward***
Klosters Rederi A/S, Oslo

Builders: CN del Tirreno &
Riuniti, Riva Trigoso
Yard no: 288
16,607 GRT; 160.0 × 22.8 m /
525 × 74.8 ft; FIAT diesels;
18,000 BHP; Twin screw; 21.5 kn;
Passengers: 918 in one class;
Crew: 250.

**1971** Jun 5: Launched.
Dec: Completed.
14-day cruises from Miami in the
Caribbean.

**1-3** *The cruise liners* Starward *(1),*
Skyward *(2) and* Southward *(3)*
*entered the Caribbean cruise service*
*for Klosters Rederi A/S.*

1

2

3

# Royal Caribbean Cruise Liners

Motorship *Song of Norway*
Royal Caribbean Cruise Line, Oslo

Builders: Wärtsilä, Helsinki
Yard no: 392
18,416 GRT; 168.3 × 24.0 m /
552 × 78.7 ft; Sulzer geared
diesels from builders; Twin screw;
18,000 BHP; 21 kn; Passengers:
724 in one class; Crew: 320.

**1969** Dec 2: Launched.
**1970** Oct 5: Delivered.
Owners: I.M. Skaugen, Oslo.
Nov 7: Maiden cruise from Miami.
The *Song of Norway* was built
specifically for Caribbean cruising.

Motorship *Nordic Prince*
Royal Caribbean Cruise Line, Oslo

Builders: Wärtsilä, Helsinki
Yard no: 393
18,436 GRT; 168.3 × 24.0 m /
552 × 78.7 ft; Sulzer geared
diesels from builders; Twin screw;
18,000 BHP; 21 kn; Passengers:
714 in one class; Crew: 320.

**1970** Jul 9: Launched.
**1971** Jul 8: Delivered. Owners: A.
Wilhelmsen, Oslo.
Cruising from Miami in the
Caribbean.
Jul 31: First cruise.

Motorship *Sun Viking*
Royal Caribbean Cruise Line, Oslo

Builders: Wärtsilä, Helsinki
Yard no: 394
18,559 GRT; 171.6 × 24.0 m /
563 × 78.7 ft; Sulzer geared
diesels from builders; Twin screw;
18,000 BHP; 21 kn; Passengers:
728 in one class; Crew: 320.

**1971** Nov 27: Launched.
**1972** Nov 10: Delivered. Owners:
I.M. Skaugen, Oslo.,
Dec 9: Maiden cruise in the
Caribbean from Miami.

**1-3** *From 1970 to 1972 the Finnish
Wärtsilä shipyard delivered the three
cruise liners* Song of Norway *(1),*
Nordic Prince *(2) and* Sun Viking *(3)
to the Royal Caribbean Cruise Line.*

1

2

3

# Blenheim and Boheme

Motorship *Blenheim*
F. Olsen Ltd, London

Builders: Upper Clyde, Govan
Yard no: 744
10,420 GRT; 149.2 × 20.6 m /
489 × 67.6 ft; Crossley-
Pielstick geared diesels; Twin
screw; 18,000 BHP; 21, max over
23 kn; Passengers: 396 in one class
(995 in ferry service); Crew: 130;
300 cars.

**1970** Jan 10: Launched.
Sep 1: Delivered.
Summer service between London
and Las Palmas.
Cruising during the winter
months.

Motorship *Boheme*
Wallenius Bremen GmbH,
Bremen

Builders: Wärtsilä, Turku
Yard no: 1161
10,328 GRT; 134.3 × 21.0 m /
441 × 68.9 ft; Sulzer diesels from
builders; Twin screw; 14,000 BHP;
21, max 23 kn; Passengers: 460 in
one class.

**1968** Feb 12: Launched.
Nov 12: Delivered. 9,866 GRT.
Used exclusively for cruising
mainly from US ports.
**1970** 10,328 GRT.

1

1 *The* Blenheim *was built for the London-Las Palmas service.*
2 *The motorship* Boheme *of Wallenius Bremen GmbH.*

Motorship *Sea Venture*
Norwegian Cruiseships A/S, Oslo

1975 *Pacific Princess*

Builders: Nordseewerke, Emden
Yard no: 411
19,903 GRT; 168.8 × 24.6 m /
554 × 80.7 ft; FIAT geared
diesels; Twin screw; 18,000 BHP;
20, max 21.5 kn; Passengers: 767
in one class; Crew: 317.

**1970** May 9: Launched.
**1971** May 8: Private cruise.
May 14: Named and delivered at
Oslo.
Jun: Maiden cruise New
York-Hamilton under the
management of Flagship Cruises
Ltd.
**1972** Sep: Taken over by O.
Lorentzen, Oslo. Previously, she
was under the joint ownership of
the Norwegian shipping
companies Lorentzen and
Fearnley & Eger.
**1974** Oct: Sold to P & O Line,
London, with delivery in April
1975.
**1975** Apr: Renamed *Pacific
Princess*.
Cruising from US ports; in winter
from Australian ports.

Motorship *Island Venture*
Norwegian Cruiseships A/S, Oslo

1972 *Island Princess*

Builders: Nordseewerke, Emden
*Yard no: 414*
19,907 GRT; 168.8 × 24.6 m /
554 × 80.7 ft; FIAT geared
diesels; Twin screw; 18,000 BHP;
20, max 21.5 kn; Passengers: 767
in one class; Crew: 317.

**1971** Mar 6: Launched.
Nov 20: Trials.
Dec 14: The ship named at Oslo.
**1972** Jan 4: Delivered.
Cruising between New York and
Hamilton under the management
of Flagship Cruises.
Sep: Taken over by Fearnley &
Eger, Oslo, having been
previously under the joint
ownership of Lorentzen and
Fearnley & Eger. Renamed *Island
Princess*. Cruising from US ports.
**1974** Aug: Sold to P & O Line,
London. Continued cruising from
US ports.

**1-3** *Nordseewerke Emden built the
cruise ships* Sea Venture *(1/2) and*
Island Venture *(3).*

1

2

3

# Dubigeon Ferries

Motorship *Eagle*
Southern Ferries Ltd (P & O),
London

1975 *Azur*

Builders: Dubigeon-Normandie
SA, Nantes
Yard no: 123
11,609 GRT; 141.8 × 22.6 m /
465 × 74.1 ft; Pielstick geared
diesels, L'Atlantique; Twin screw;
20,400 BHP; 22, max 23.3 kn;
Passengers: 750 in one class;
Crew: 138; 200 cars.

**1970** Oct 16: Launched.
**1971** Apr 22: Trials.
May 16: Delivered.
May 18: Maiden voyage
Southampton-Lisbon-Tangier.
**1975** Oct: To Nouvelle Cie de
Paquebots, Marseille. Renamed
*Azur*. Ferry service in
Mediterranean. Cruising.

Motorship *Massalia*
Nouvelle Cie de Paquebots
(Chargeurs Réunis); Marseille

Builders: Dubigeon-Normandie
SA, Nantes
Yard no: 124
10,513 GRT; 141.8 × 21.9 m /
465 × 71.8 ft; Pielstick geared
diesels, L'Atlantique; Twin screw;
16,000 BHP; 21 kn; Passengers:
494 1st class; 316 tourist class;
Crew: 84; 260 cars, 36 lorries.

**1971** Jan 19: Launched.
Jul: Completed.
Marseille-Casablanca-Canary
Islands service.

1-3 *The Dubigeon-Normandie
shipbuilders developed a highly
successful ocean-going class of deep-
sea ferry.* (1) *shows the British* Eagle,
(2) *the French* Massalia *and* (3) *the
Norwegian* Bolero.

Motorship *Bolero*
F. Olsen, Oslo

Builders: Dubigeon-Normandie
SA, Nantes
Yard no: 133
11,344 GRT; 142.1 × 21.9 m /
466 × 71.8 ft; Pielstick geared
diesels, L'Atlantique; Twin screw;
20,400 BHP; 21, max 23 kn;
Passengers: 967 in one class;
Crew: 140; 250 cars.

**1972** Jun 13: Launched.
**1973** Feb: Completed.
The *Bolero* did not sail between
Travemünde-Södertälje as
originally intended but was placed
instead in the Bremerhaven/
Hamburg-Harwich service. In
March she went to the USA to be
used in the Portland-Yarmouth
service. Cruising during the
winter.
**1976** Oslo-Newcastle service.

1

2

3

Motorship *Spirit of London*
P & O Line, London

*1974 Sun Princess*

Builders: CN del Tirreno &
Riuniti, Riva Trigoso
Yard no: R 290
17,370 GRT; 163.3 × 22.8 m /
536 × 74.8 ft; FIAT geared
diesels; Twin screw; 18,000 BHP;
20.5, max 21.95 kn; Passengers:
874; Crew: 322.

**1972** Apr 29: Launched.
Originally ordered by the
Norwegian Klosters Rederi, from
whom P & O took over the
contract in 1971.
Aug: Completed.
Sep: Delivered.
Nov 11: Maiden voyage
Southampton-San Juan. Then
cruising on the US West Coast.
**1974** Oct: Renamed *Sun
Princess*.

**1** *The* Spirit of London *was the first
P & O passenger vessel built
exclusively for cruising.*
**2/3** *The Cunard cruise liners* Cunard
Ambassador *(2) and* Cunard
Adventurer *(3) came from Dutch
yards.*

Motorship *Cunard Adventurer*
Cunard Line, Southampton

Builders: Rotterdamsche DD Mij
Yard no: 329
14,151 GRT; 147.5 × 21.6 m /
484 × 70.8 ft; Stork-Werkspoor
geared diesels; Twin screw; 28,000
BHP; 22, max 24 kn; Passengers:
832 in one class; Crew: 412.

**1971** Feb 2: Launched. Ordered
by Overseas National Airways Inc,
in which Cunard had a 50%
share. In July 1970 Cunard took
over ONA in its entirety.
Aug 28: Trials.
Oct 19: Delivered.
Nov 19: Maiden voyage
Southampton-San Juan. Then
Caribbean cruising.
**1976** Sold to Klosters Rederi
A/S, Oslo.

Motorship *Cunard Ambassador*
Cunard Line, Southampton

*1975 Linda Clausen*

Builders: P. Smit jr, Rotterdam
Yard no: 666
14,160 GRT; 148.1 × 21.5 kn;
Stork-Werkspoor geared diesels;
Twin screw; 28,000 BHP; 22, max

24 kn; Passengers: 831 in one
class; Crew: 410.

**1972** Mar 16: Launched. As in
the case of her sister ship, the
*Cunard Ambassador* also had
been ordered by ONA, which
became 100 per cent Cunard-
owned in July 1970.
Oct 21: Delivered.
Oct 23: Maiden voyage
Southampton-San Juan, then
Caribbean cruising.
**1974** Sep 12: During a voyage
without passengers from Port
Everglades to New Orleans a fire
broke out in the engine room and
soon spread to several decks.
Sep 15: Towed into Key West by
the salvage tug *Cable*.
**1975** Declared a total loss. Sold
to C. Clausen D/S A/S in
Copenhagen.
Mar: Renamed *Linda Clausen*.
Apr 30: Towed to Landskrona by
the *Willem Barendsz*. Rebuilt
there as a livestock transport for
service between Australia and the
Persian Gulf.
**1976** Jan: To Hamburg for
further rebuilding.
Jun 15: Left Hamburg after
completion.

1

2

3

# The Royal Viking Class

Motorship *Royal Viking Star*
Royal Viking Line, Bergen

Builders: Wärtsilä, Helsinki
Yard no: 395
21,847 GRT; 177.7 × 25.2 m /
583 × 82.7 ft; Sulzer geared
diesels from builders; Twin screw;
18,000 BHP; 21.5 kn; Passengers:
539 in one class; Crew: 326.

**1971** May 12: Launched.
**1972** Jun 26: Delivered. Owner:
Det Bergenske D/S, Bergen.
Worldwide cruising.

*1-3 The three new Wärtsilä ships of
the Royal Viking class:* Royal Viking
Star (*1*), Royal Viking Sky (*2*) *and*
Royal Viking Sea (*3*).

Motorship *Royal Viking Sky*
Royal Viking Line, Trondheim

Builders: Wärtsilä, Helsinki
Yard no: 396
21,891 GRT; 177.7 × 25.2 m /
583 × 82.7 ft; Sulzer geared
diesels from builders; Twin screw;
18,000 BHP; 21.5 kn; Passengers:
536; Crew: 324.

**1972** May 25: Launched.
**1973** Jun 5: Delivered. Owners:
Det Nordenfjeldske D/S,
Trondheim. Worldwide cruising.

Motorship *Royal Viking Sea*
Royal Viking Line

Builders: Wärtsilä, Helsinki
Yard no: 397
21,848 GRT; 177.7 × 25.2 m /
583 × 82.7 ft; Sulzer geared
diesels from builders; Twin screw;
18,000 BHP; 21.5 kn; Passengers:
536; Crew: 324.

**1973** Jan 19: Launched.
Nov 16: Delivered. Owners: A.F.
Klaveness & Co A/S.
Nov 25: Maiden voyage Bergen-
Newcastle as a replacement for
the *Leda*, which was under repair.
Dec: Worldwide cruising.

1

2

3

# The Princess of Acadia

Motorship *Princess of Acadia*
Canadian Pacific, St John

Launched as *Princess of Nova*

Builders: St John SB & DD Co
Yard no: 98
10,109 GRT; 146.3 × 20.5 m /
480 × 67.2 ft; General Motors
geared diesels; Twin screw; 11,500

BHP; 18.75, max over 20 kn;
Passengers: 650 in one class;
Crew: 42; 159 cars.

**1971** Launched.
May 15: Completed.
May 27: Maiden voyage in New
Brunswick-Nova Scotia service
across the Bay of Fundy.

**1974** Sold to the Canadian
Government.

**1** *The* Princess of Acadia *was built for
Bay of Fundy service.*

1

Motorship *Sun Flower*
Nippon Kosoku Ferry Co Ltd,
Tokyo

Builders: Kawasaki, Kobe
Yard no: 1158
11,312 GRT, 185.0 × 24.0 m /
607 × 78.7 ft; MAN geared
diesels from builders; Twin screw;
26,080 BHP; 24, max 25.5 kn;
Passengers: 1,124 in one class;
Crew: 87; 208 cars, 84 lorries.

**1971** Sep 6: Launched.
**1972** Jan 18: Delivered.
Feb 1: Maiden voyage in Nagoya-
Kagoshima ferry service.

Motorship *Sun Flower 2*
Nippon Kosoku Ferry Co Ltd,
Tokyo

Launched as *Sun Rise*

Builders: Kawasaki, Kobe
Yard no: 1159
11,314 GRT; 185.0 × 24.0 m /
607 × 78.7 ft; MAN geared
diesels from builders; Twin screw;
26,080 BHP; 24, max 25.5 kn;
Passengers: 1,110 in one class;
Crew: 87; 208 cars, 84 lorries.

**1972** Jan 18: Launched as *Sun
Rise*, but renamed *Sun Flower 2*

during the fitting-out.
May 17: Delivered.
May 28: Maiden voyage in
Nagoya-Kagoshima ferry service.

**1** *The sister ships* Sun Flower *(1) and*
Sun Flower 2 *(2) are two of the fastest
and most modern car ferries in the
world.*

**1**

**2**

Motorship *Sun Flower 5*
Nippon Kosoku Ferry Co Ltd,
Tokyo

Builders: Kurushima Dock Co,
Imabari
Yard no: 730
12,711 GRT; 185.0 × 24.0 m /
607 × 78.7 ft; MAN geared
diesels; Kawasaki; Twin screw;
26,080 BHP; 24, max 25.5 kn;
Passengers: 1,079 in one class;
Crew: 87; 97 cars, 100 lorries.
**1972** Launched.
**1973** Mar 3: Completed.
Mar 21: Maiden voyage Tokyo-
Kochi.

Motorship *Sun Flower 8*
Nippon Kosoku Ferry Co Ltd,
Tokyo

Builders: Kurushima Dock Co,
Imabari
Yard no: 731
12,759 GRT; 185.0 × 24.0 m /
607 × 78.7 ft; MAN geared
diesels, Kawasaki; Twin screw;
26,080 BHP; 24, max 25.5 kn;
Passengers: 1,079 in one class;
Crew: 87; 92 cars, 100 lorries.

**1973** Launched.
Jun 25: Completed.
Jul 4: Maiden voyage Tokyo-
Kochi.

Motorship *Sun Flower 11*
Nippon Kosoku Ferry Co Ltd,
Tokyo

Builders: Kurushima Dock Co,
Imabari
Yard no: 775
13,598 GRT; 195.0 × 24.0 m /
640 × 78.7 ft; MAN diesels,
Kawasaki; Twin screw; 36,000
BHP; 25, max 26.85 kn;
Passengers: 1,124 in one class;
Crew: 87; 192 cars, 85 lorries.

**1974** Apr 23: Launched.
Sep 9: Delivered.
Osaka-Kagoshima service.

3

4

5

**Motorship *Ferry Akashia***
Shinnihonkai Ferry Co Ltd, Otaru

Builders: Kanda SB Co,
Yard no: 178
11,210 GRT; 180.5 × 26.4 m /
592 × 86.6 ft; MAN diesels,
Kawasaki; Twin screw; 23,000
BHP; 23, max 25.3 kn;
Passengers: 1,387 in one class;
119 lorries, 150 cars.

**1973** Mar 1: Launched.
Jul 14: Delivered.
Jul 21: Maiden voyage in
Tsuruga-Otaru ferry service.

6

**Motorship *Sapporo Maru***
Nippon Enkai Car Ferry

Builders: Hayashikane Shosen
KK, Shimonoseki
Yard no: 1177
11,097 GRT; 164.0 × 24.0 m /
538 × 78.7 ft; MAN diesels,
Mitsubishi; Twin screw; 28,000
BHP; 22.25, max 24.25 kn;
Passengers: 808.

**1974** Apr 9: Launched.
Jul: Completed.
Aug 2: Maiden voyage Tokyo-
Tomakomai.

7

**3-7** *More purpose-built Japanese
ferries:* Sun Flower 5 (*3*), Sun Flower 8
(*4*), Sun Flower 11 (*5*), Ferry Akashia
(*6*) *and* Sapporo Maru (*7*).

# New Ships for the Congo Service

Motorship *Fabiolaville*
Compagnie Maritime Belge, Antwerp

Builders: Cockerill, Hoboken
Yard no: 861
13,303 GRT; 161.2 × 23.1 m / 529 × 75.8 ft; Burmeister & Wain diesels, Cockerill; Single screw; 15,040 BHP; 20 kn; Passengers: 71 in one class; Crew: 58.

**1972** Jan 28: Launched.
May 15-18: Trials.
Jun 2: Delivered.
Jun: Hamburg-Antwerp-Matadi service.

Motorship *Kananga*
Cie Mar Congolaise, Matadi

Builders: Cockerill, Hoboken
Yard no: 862
13,481 GRT; 161.2 × 23.1 m / 529 × 75.8 ft; Burmeister & Wain diesels, Cockerill; Single screw; 15,040 BHP; 20 kn; Passengers: 71 in one class; Crew: 58.

**1972** Aug 24: Launched.
**1973** Jan 29-Feb 1: Trials.
Feb 9: Delivered.
Feb 15: Maiden voyage Antwerp-Matadi.
**1975** Nov 15: Following a collision with the Soviet trawler *Youzas Garyalis* west of the Ile de Sein the *Kananga* appeared to tbe sinking. Passengers and part of the crew left the ship which was eventually brought into Brest on November 16 by the tug *Baltic*.

**1/ 2** *The combi-ships* Fabiolaville (*1*) *and* Kananga (*2*).

Motorship *Copenhagen*
A/S Nordline, Copenhagen

1975 *Odessa*

Builders: Vickers, Barrow
Yard no: 1085
13,758 GRT; 136.0 × 21.5 m /
446 × 70.5 ft; Pielstick geared
diesels, Crossley; Twin screw;
16,000 BHP; 19 kn; Passengers:
600.

**1970** The incomplete ship was
offered for sale while still on the
stocks because of a disagreement
between the shipping company
and the builders concerning high
additional costs.
**1971** Sep: A/S Nordline and
Vickers came to an agreement
over continuing the building of the
ship. Intended name: *Prins Henrik
af Danmark*.
**1972** Dec 20: Launched but not
named.
**1973** Mar 27: Towed from
Barrow to Newcastle, where Swan
Hunter took over the completion.
**1974** Mar: First trials.
Apr: Nordline, which had run into
financial difficulties, put the
*Copenhagen* up for sale.
**1975** May: Sold to the Soviet
Union, Black Sea SS Co, Odessa.
Renamed *Odessa*.
Jul 18: Handing over voyage
Liverpool-Leningrad. Cruising.

Motorship *Dana Regina*
Det Forenede D/S, Copenhagen

Builders: Aalborg Vaerft
Yard no: 200
12,192 GRT; 152.5 × 22.7 m /
500 × 74.5 ft; Burmeister &
Wain geared diesels; Twin screw;
19,360 BHP; 21 kn; Passengers:
878; 100 lorries, 250 cars; Crew:
185.

**1973** Aug 31: Launched
unnamed.
**1974** Jul: Named and delivered.
Cruise to London.
Jul 9: Maiden voyage in Esbjerg-
Harwich service.

**1/2** *The new Danish ships*
Copenhagen (*1*) *and* Dana Regina,
*completed in 1974.*

1

2

Motorship *Monte Toledo*
Naviera Aznar, Bilbao

Builders: Union Naval de
Levante, Valencia
Yard no: 129
10,851 GRT; 151.5 × 20.7 m /
497 × 67.9 ft; MAN geared
diesels, Bazan; Twin screw;
17,800 BHP; 21, max over 23 kn;
Passengers: 798 in one class, (388
when cruising); Crew: 130, (160
when cruising); 300 cars.

**1973** Mar 10: Launched.
**1974** Feb 14: Trials.
Santander-Southampton service.
Cruising in winter.
Mar: Maiden voyage Valencia-
London.

Motorship *Monte Granada*
Naviera Aznar, Bilbao

Builders: Union Naval de Levante,
Valencia
Yard no: 130
10,829 GRT; 151.5 × 20.7 m /
497 × 67.9 ft; MAN geared
diesels, Bazan; Twin screw;
17,800 BHP; 21, max over 23 kn;
Passengers: 798 (388 when
cruising) in one class; Crew: 130,
(160 when cruising); 300 cars.

**1974** Feb 9: Launched.
**1975** Oct 7: Maiden voyage
Liverpool-Canary Islands.
Amsterdam-Southampton-
Santander service during winter
months.

*1/2 Launch (1) and trials (2) of the*
Monte Toledo.
*3 The* Monte Granada *berthing at
Liverpool on October 6 1975.*

1

# North Sea Ferries

Motorship *Norland*
North Sea Ferries Ltd, Hull

Builders: AG 'Weser', Seebeck
yard, Bremerhaven
Yard no: 972
12,988 GRT; 153.0 × 25.2 m /
502 × 82.7 ft; Werkspoor diesels;
Twin screw; 18,000 BHP; 18.5 kn;
1,066 passengers in cabins, 177
unberthed; Crew: 98.

**1973** Oct 13: Launched.
**1974** Jun 7: Delivered.
Ferry service Hull-Rotterdam.

Motorship *Norstar*
Noordzee Veerdiensten,
Rotterdam

Builders: AG 'Weser', Seebeck
yard, Bremerhaven
Yard no: 973
12,502 GRT; 153.0 × 25.2 m /
502 × 82.7 ft; Werkspoor diesels;
Twin screw; 18,000 BHP; 18.5 kn;
1,070 passengers in cabins, 173
unberthed; Crew: 98.

**1974** Jul 5: Launched.
Dec 14: Delivered.
Rotterdam-Hull ferry service.

**1** *In June 1974 the Seebeck shipyard
delivered the* Norland, *the first of two
sister ships for the Rotterdam-Hull
ferry service.*

1

2

Motorship *Peter Pan*
TT-Line GmbH & Co, Lübeck

Builders: Werft Nobiskrug,
Rendsburg
Yard no: 681
12,528 GRT; 149.4 × 24.0 m /
490 × 78.7 ft; Pielstick geared
diesels, OEW; Twin screw;
20,800 BHP; 22 kn; 1,600
passengers, 712 in cabins; Crew:
125; 470 cars or 45 lorries.

**1974** Feb 2: Launched.
May 22: Delivered. Baltic Sea
cruise.
May 25: Maiden voyage in
Travemünde-Trelleborg ferry
service.
Cruising in winter.

Motorship *Nils Holgersson*
TT-Line GmbH & Co, Lübeck

Builders: Nobiskrug, Rendsburg
Yard no: 682
12,527 GRT; 149.4 × 24.0 m /
490 × 78.7 ft; Pielstick geared
disels, OEW; Twin screw; 20,800
BHP; 22 kn; 1,600 passengers, 712
in cabins; Crew: 125; 470 cars or
45 lorries.

**1974** Oct 26: Launched.
**1975** Apr 8: Delivered.
After a maiden cruise from
Travemünde to Gothenburg and
Oslo the ship entered the
Travemünde-Trelleborg ferry
service. Cruising in winter.

1 *The* Peter Pan, *delivered in May
1974. When she entered service she
was the largest ferry on the Baltic Sea.*
2 *The* Nils Holgersson *leaving
Travemünde.*

1

2

Motorship *El-Djazair*
CN Algérienne de Nav, Algiers

Ex *Central No. 3*

Builders: Kanasashi Zosensho,
Shimizu
Yard no: 965
12,529 GRT; 130.4 × 22.0 m /
428 × 72.2 ft; MAN diesels,
Kawasaki; Twin screw; 15,200
BHP; 19.5 kn; Passengers: 8 1st
class, 548 2nd class and lorry
drivers, 300 unberthed; 99 lorries,
22 cars.

**1971** Mar 26: Launched as
*Central No. 3* for the Central Co,
Kobe.
Jul 22: Delivered. 5,647 GRT.
**1973** Bought by Cie Nat
Algérienne de Nav, Algiers.
Renamed *El-Djazair.* Marseille-
Algiers-Oran service.
**1974** 12,529 GRT.

Motorship *Tassili*
CN Algérienne de Nav, Algiers

Ex *Central No. 1*

Builders: Mitsubishi, Shimonoseki
Yard no: 688
10,223 GRT; 128.3 × 22.0 m /
421 × 72.2 ft; Diesels, Mitsubishi;
15,000 BHP; Twin screw; 19.5 kn;
Passengers: 59 1st class, 416 2nd
class, 80 drivers, 300 unberthed;
20 cars, 130 lorries.

**1970** Nov 14: Launched as *Central
No. 1* for the Central Ferry Co,
Kobe.
**1971** Mar 29: Delivered. 5,744
GRT. Kobe-Tokyo service.
**1973** Bought by the Cie Nat
Algérienne de Nav, Algiers.
Renamed *Tassili.*
Marseille-Algiers-Oran service.
**1974** 10,233 GRT.

1/2 *The Algerian national shipping
company bought two Japanese ferries
in 1973 and placed them in
Mediterranean service after having
them rebuilt.* (1) *shows the* El-
Djazair *and* (2) *shows the* Tassili
*while she was still the Japanese* Central
No. 1.

Motorship *Svea Corona*
Stockholms Rederi A/B Svea,
Stockholm

Builders: Dubigeon-Normandie,
Nantes
Yard no: 141
12,576 GRT; 152.1 × 22. 3 m /
499 × 73.1 ft; Pielstick geared
diesels, Atlantique; Twin screw;
24,000 BHP; 22 kn; Passengers:
800 in one class, 400 unberthed;
Crew: 150; 290 cars.

**1974** Jul 19: Launched.
**1975** Delivered.
Helsinki-Stockholm service.

Motorship *Wellamo*
Finska Angfartygs, Helsinki

Builders: Dubigeon-Normandie,
Nantes
Yard no: 142
12,348 GRT; 153.1 × 22.3 m /
499 × 73.1 ft; Pielstick geared
diesels, Atlantique; Twin screw;
24,000 BHP; 22 kn; Passengers:
799 in one class, 401 unberthed;
Crew: 150; 290 cars.

**1974** Nov: Launched.
**1975** Delivered.
Helsinki-Stockholm service.

*1-3 Three Scandinavian shipping
companies are running a service
between Helsinki and Stockholm
under the title of Silja Line,
commissioning in 1975 the three new
ships* Bore Star *(1),* Svea Corona *(2)
and* Wellamo *(3).*

Motorship *Bore Star*
Bore Angfartygs, Åbo

Builders: Dubigeon-Normandie,
Nantes
yard no: 143
12,343 GRT; 153. 1 × 22.3 m /
499 × 73.1 ft; Pielstick geared
diesels, Atlantique; Twin screw;
24,000 BHP; 22 kn; Passengers:
658 in one class, 400 unberthed;
Crew: 150; 290 cars.

**1975** Jan 30: Launched.
Dec: Delivered.
Dec 11: Maiden cruise West
Africa-Cherbourg.
Helsinki-Stockholm service from
May to October.

*4 The* Ishikari, *sister ship to the*
Daisetsu.

1

2

3

4

Motorship *Ishikari*
Teiheiyo Enkai Ferry KK, Nagoya

Builders: Nakai Zosen KK, Setoda
Yard no: 387
11,300 GRT; 175.6 × 24.0 m /
576 × 78.7 ft; MAN diesels,
Mitsubishi; Twin screw; 27,580
BHP; 23.5, max 26.06 kn;
Passengers: 905 in one class; 130
lorries, 105 cars.

**1974** Sep 19: Launched.
Dec 23: Delivered.
Nagoya-Ohita (Kyushu) service.
**1975** Nagoya-Sendai-Tomakomai
service.

Motorship *Cunard Countess*
Cunard Line, Southampton

Builders: Burmeister & Wain,
Copenhagen
Yard no: 858
17,586 GRT; 163.0 × 22.8 m /
535 × 74.8 ft; Burmeister & Wain
geared diesels; Twin screw; 21,000
BHP; 21.5 kn; Passengers: 800 in
one class.

**1974** Sep 20: Launched.
**1975** May 21: Delivered.
May 28: Arrived at La Spezia for
internal fitting by Industrie Navali
Mechaniche Affini.
**1976** July: Completed.
Aug 14: First cruise from San
Juan, Puerto Rico.

Motorship *Tor Britannia*
Tor Line A/B, Gothenburg

Builders: Flender Werft, Lübeck
Yard no: 607
15,657 GRT; 182.4 × 23.7 m /
590 × 77.7 ft; Pielstick geared
diesels, Lindholmens; Twin screw;
41,600 BHP; 24.5, max 26 kn;
Passengers: 756 in cabins, 512
couchettes, 273 unberthed; 500
when cruising; Crew: 143; 420
cars.

**1974** Oct 10: Launched.
**1975** May 16: Delivered.
Gothenburg-Felixstowe service.
May 22: Arrived at Felixtowe for
the first time.
**1976** Gothenburg-Immingham
service.

Motorship *Daisetsu*
Teiheiyo Enkai Ferry KK, Nagoya

Builders: Nakai Zosen KK, Setoda
Yard no: 388
11,879 GRT; 175.6 × 24.0 m /
576 × 78.7 ft; MAN diesels,
Mitsubishi; Twin screw; 27,580
BHP; 23.5 kn; Passengers: 900 in
one class; 130 lorries, 105 cars.

**1975** Mar 28: Launched.
Jun 20: Delivered.
Nagoya-Sendai-Tomakomai
service.

Motorship *Cunard Conquest*
Cunard Line, Southampton

1976 *Cunard Princess*

Builders: Burmeister & Wain,
Copenhagen
Yard no: 859
17,586 GRT; 163.0 × 22.8 m /
535 × 74.8 ft; Burmeister & Wain
geared diesels; Twin screw; 21,000
BHP; 21.5 kn; Passengers: 800 in
one class.

**1974** Dec: Launched.
**1975** Oct 30: Delivered.
Nov 6: Arrived at La Spezia for
internal fitting by Industrie Navali
Mechaniche Affini.
**1976** Renamed *Cunard Princess*.

Motorship *Tor Scandinavia*
Tor Line A/B, Gothenburg

Builders: Flender Werft, Lübeck
Yard no: 608
15,673 GRT; 182.4 × 23.7 m /
590 × 77.7 ft; Pielstick geared
diesels, Lindholmen; Twin screw;
41,600 BHP; 24.5 kn; Passengers:
756 in cabins, 512 couchettes, 273
unberthed, 500 when cruising;
Crew: 143; 420 cars.

**1975** Nov 4: Launched.
**1976** Apr 12: Delivered.
Gothenburg-Felixstowe service.

**1** *The* Cunard Countess *at her
Burmeister & Wain fitting-out berth.
She and her sister ship were ordered
for worldwide cruising.*
**2** *Europe's largest ferries are the* Tor
Britannia *(2) and* Tor Scandinavia,
*ultra-modern ships with distinctive
lines.*

Motorship *Belorussiya*
USSR, Odessa (Black Sea SS Co)

Builders: Wärtsilä, Turku
Yard no: 1212
16,631 GRT; 157.0 × 21.8 m /
515 × 71.5 ft; Pielstick geared
diesels; Twin screw; 18,000 BHP;
22 kn; Passengers: 504 in cabins,
114 in reclining seats, 391
unberthed, 350 when cruising;
Crew: 191; 256 cars, 23 lorries.

**1974** Mar 6: Launched.
**1975** Jan 15: Delivered.
Cruising in European waters.

Motorship *Azerbaydzhan*
USSR, Odessa (Black Sea SS Co)

Builders: Wärtsilä, Turku
Yard no: 1221
16,631 GRT; 157.0 × 21.8 m /
515 × 71.5 ft; Pielstick geared
diesels; Twin screw; 18,000 BHP;
22 kn; Passengers: 504 in cabins,
114 in reclining seats, 390
unberthed, 350 when cruising;
Crew: 191; 256 cars, 23 lorries.

**1975** Apr 4: Launched.
Dec 18: Launched.
Cruising in European waters.

Motorship *Kareliya*
USSR, Odessa (Black Sea SS Co)

Builders: Wärtsilä, Turku
Yard no: 1223
16,631 GRT; 157.0 × 21.9 m /
515 × 71.5 ft; Pielstick geared
diesels; Twin screw; 18,000 BHP;
22 kn; Passengers: 504 in cabins,
114 in reclining seats, 391
unberthed. 350 when cruising;
Crew: 191; 256 cars, 23 lorries.

**1976** Apr 14: Launched.
Dec: Delivered.
Cruising.

Motorship *Gruziya*
USSR, Odessa (Black Sea SS Co)

Builders: Wärtsilä, Turku
Yard no: 1213
16,631 GRT; 157.0 × 21.8 m /
515 × 71.5 ft; Pielstick geared
diesels; Twin screw; 18,000 BHP;
22 kn; Passengers: 505 in cabins,
114 in reclining seats, 391
unberthed, 350 when cruising;
Crew: 191; 256 cars, 23 lorries.

**1974** Oct 18: Launched.
**1975** Jun 30: Delivered.
Cruising in European waters.

Motorship *Kazakhstan*
USSR, Odessa (Black Sea SS Co)

Builders: Wärtsilä, Turku
Yard no: 1222
16,631 GRT; 157.0 × 21.9 m /
515 × 71.5 ft; Pielstick geared
diesels; Twin screw; 18,000 BHP;
22 kn; Passengers: 504 in cabins,
114 in reclining seats, 391
unberthed. 350 when cruising;
Crew: 191; 256 cars, 23 lorries.

**1975** Oct 17: Launched.
**1976** Jun: Delivered.
Cruising.

*1-3 The order for five fast ferry/cruise
vessels underlines the forced expansion
which has been taking place in the
Soviet passenger ship fleet in recent
years. (1) shows the prototype ship of
the class, the* Belorussiya, *(2) the*
Gruziya *and (3) the* Azerbaydzhan.

1

Motorship *Daphne*
J.C. Carras, Piraeus

Ex *Akrotiri Express*
Ex *Port Sydney*

Builders: Swan, Hunter &
Wigham Richardson, Newcastle
Yard no: 1827
16,310 GRT; 162.4 × 21.4 m /
533 × 70.2 ft; Doxford diesels,
Wallsend Slipway; Twin screw;
13,200 BHP; 17 kn; Passengers:
503 in one class.

**1954** Oct 29: Launched as cargo
liner *Port Sydney* for the Port Line,
London.
**1955** Mar: Completed. 11,683
GRT. 12 passengers 1st class.
London-Australia-New Zealand
service.
**1972** Sold to J.C. Carras.
Registered as the *Akrotiri Express*
for the Akrotiri Express Shipping
Co. Rebuilt as a cruise liner at the
Chalkis yard in Greece.
**1975** Renamed *Daphne*.
Jun: Trials after rebuilding.
Jul 26: First cruise from Marseille.
**1976** Registered for Delian Athina
Cruises SA. 10,545 GRT.

Motorship *Danae*
J.C. Carras, Piraeus

Ex *Therisos Express*
Ex *Port Melbourne*

Builders: Harland & Wolff,
Belfast
Yard no: 1483
approx. 16,300 GRT; 162. 4 ×
21.4 m / 533 × 70.2 ft;
Burmeister & Wain diesels, H &
W; Twin screw; 13,200 BHP; 17
kn; Passengers: 512 in one class.

**1955** Mar 10: Launched as cargo
liner *Port Melbourne* for the Port
Line, London.
Jul: Completed. 10,205 GRT. 12
passengers 1st class.
London-Australia-New Zealand
service; occasionally South Africa-
New Zealand.
**1972** Bought by J.C. Carras.
Registered as *Therisos Express* for
the Therisos Express Shipping Co.
Rebuilt as a passenger ship at the
Chalkis yard in Greece.
**1975** Renamed *Danae*.
**1976** Registered for Delian Athina
Cruises SA. 12,123 GRT.
Cruising.

Motorship *Kronprins Harald*
Anders Jahre, Sandefjord

Builders: Nobiskrug, Rendsburg
Yard no: 685
12,750 GRT; 156.4 × 23.5 m /
513 × 77.1 ft; Werkspoor geared
diesels; Twin screw; 24,000 BHP;
22.5 kn; Passengers: 585 1st class,
415 tourist class; Crew: 138; 404
cars.

**1975** Oct 4: Launched.
**1976** Mar 30: Delivered.
Apr 2: Maiden voyage Oslo-Kiel.

Motorship *Napoleon*
CGT Méditerranée, Marseille

Builders: Dubigeon-Normandie,
Nantes
Yard no: 156
14,918 GRT; 155.0 × 24.0 m /
508 × 78.7 ft; Pielstick geared
diesels; Twin screw; 18,000 BHP;
23.5 kn; 1,907 passengers.

**1975** Nov 4: Launched.
**1976** Mar: CGT-Méditerranée
was reorganised as the SNCM
(Société Nationale Maritime
Corse-Méditerranée), Marseille.
Jun 21: Maiden voyage Marseille-
Ajaccio-Toulon.

1

2

**1** *The* Daphne *and* Danae *were
converted from refrigerated ships to
cruise liners.*
**2** *The ferry* Kronprins Harald.

Turbine ship *Finnjet*
Finnlines O/Y, Helsinki
Builders: Wärtsilä, Helsinki
Yard no: 407
approx. 23,000 GRT; 212.8 ×
25.4 m / 692 × 83.3 ft; Pratt &
Whitney gas turbines; Twin screw;
75,000 SHP; 30.5 kn; Passengers:
1,532; 220 cars, 30 lorries.

**1976**  Mar 28: Floated in dry dock.
Dec 9: First trial trip.
Apr: Delivered.
Helsinki-Travemünde-service.

**1** *The gas turbine vessel* Finnjet *of Finnlines was undocked on March 28 1976.*

1

The following are those companies listed in alphabetical order which have owned passenger ships of 10,000 GRT and over. The titles of those still owning such ships are printed in heavy type. The location of a company's head office is not necessarily the port of registry of all or of any of its ships.

Aberdeen Line, London (George Thompson & Co Ltd)
Aberdeen & Commonwealth Line Ltd, London
**Achille Lauro, Naples**
**Admiral Oriental Line, Seattle**
**'Adriatica' SpA di Navigazione, Venice**
Africa Shipping Co Ltd, Hong Kong
Aktiengesellschaft Hugo Stinnes für Seeschiffahrt und Überseehandel, Hamburg
Allan Line Steamship Co Ltd, Glasgow
Alvion Steamship Corp, Panama (Sitmar Line)
American Banner Lines Inc, New York
American Export Isbrandtsen Lines Inc, New York
American Export Lines, New York (Isbrandtsen)
American Line, New York (American Line SS Corporation)
American Mail Line, Seattle
American Palestine Line, New York
American President Lines Ltd, San Francisco
Anchor Line (Henderson Brothers) Ltd, Glasgow (Anchor Line Ltd)
Anchor-Donaldson Ltd, Glasgow
**Aphrodite Cruises Ltd, Famagusta**
**Ares Shipping Corp, New York**
Aretusa SpA di Navigazione, Palermo
Arosa Line Inc, Geneva
Atlantic Transport Co Ltd, London
Atlantic Transport Co of West Virginia, New York
Austasia Line Ltd, Singapore
**Australian Coastal Shipping Commission, Hobart**

Balkanturist, Sofia
**Baltic Steamship Co, Leningrad**
Baltic SS Corp of America, New York
Bibby Line Ltd, Liverpool
Black & Asow Sea SS Co, Odessa
**Black Sea Steamship Co, Odessa**
Blue Funnel Line: Alfred Holt & Co, Liverpool; China Mutual SN Co Ltd, Liverpool; Ocean SS Co Ltd, Liverpool
Blue Star Line Ltd, London
Booth Steamship Co Ltd, Liverpool
**Bore Angfartygs A/B, Åbo**
**Bremer Schiffahrtsgesellschaft GmbH & Co KG, Bremen**
British India Steam Navigation Co Ltd, London
Byron Steamship Co, London

**CGT (Compagnie Générale Trans-atlantique), Paris**
Canadian Australasian Line Ltd, Vancouver
**Canadian National Railway Co, Quebec**
Canadian National Steamships, Montreal
Canadian Northern Steamships, Toronto
Canadian Pacific Steamships Ltd, London (Canadian Pacific Railway Co)
Caribbean Land & Shipping Corp, Panama
Carnival Cruise Lines Inc, Panama
**J. C. Carras, Piraeus**
**Chandris Lines, Piraeus (D. & A. Chandris)**
**Chargeurs Réunis, Compagnie Maritime des, Paris**
**China National Ocean Shipping Co, Canton**
China Navigation Co, London
**Chinese Maritime Trust Ltd, Keelung**
Cielomar SA, Panama
Cogedar Line, Genoa (Compagnia Genovese di Armamento SpA)
Commerciale Marittime Petroli SpA, Palermo
Commonwealth & Dominion Line Ltd, London (Port Line)
Commonwealth Government Line, Melbourne
Compagnie de Navigation Fraissenet et Cyprien Fabre, Marseille
Compagnie de Navigation Paquet, Marseille
Compagnie de Navigation Süd-Atlantique, Paris
Compagnie Française de Navigation, Marseille
**Compagnie Générale Maritime, Paris**
**Compagnie Maritime Belge (Lloyd Royal) SA, Antwerp**
Compagnie Maritime Congolaise, Matadi

**Compagnie Maritime du Zaire, Kinshasha**
**Compagnie National Algerienne de Navigation, Algiers**
**Compagnie Tunisienne de Navigation, Tunis**
**Companhia Colonial de Navegação, Lisbon**
Companhia Nacional de Navegação, Lisbon
Companhia Nacional de Navegação Costeira Autarquia Federal, Rio de Janeiro
**Companhia Portuguesa de Transportes Maritimos SARL, Lisbon**
Compañia Argentina de Navegaceon Dodero, Buenos Aires
**Compañia de Navegacion Abeto SA, Hong Kong**
Compañia de Navegacion Florencia SA, Panama
Compania de Navegacion Incres SA, Panama
**Compañia de Vapores Cerulea SA, Ithaka**
Compañia de Vapores Realma SA, Piraeus
Compania Naviera Tasmania, Piraeus
Compania Naviera Turistica Mexicana SA, Mexico City
Compania Transatlantica Centroameri-cana, Panama
Compañia Trasatlântica Española SA, Madrid
**Compañia Trasmediterranea, Madrid**
Coral Riviera Ltd, Tel Aviv
**Costa Armatori SpA, Genoa**
G. Costa fu Andrea, Genoa
'Cosulich' Soc Triestina di Navigazione, Trieste
**Cretan Maritime Co SA, Canea**
Crociere d'Oltremare, Cagliari
**Cunard Line Ltd, Liverpool (Cunard Steam Ship Co)**
Cunard White Star Ltd, Liverpool
Cyprien Fabre et Cie, Compagnie Française de Navigation à Vapeur, Marseille (Compagnie Générale de Navigation à Vapeur)
Czechoslovak Ocean Shipping, Prague

Delta SS Lines Inc, New Orleans
**Det Bergenske D/S, Bergen**
**Det Forenede D/S, Copenhagen**
**Det Nordenfjeldske D/S, Trondheim**
Deutsche Atlantik Linie, Hamburg
C. L. Dimon, New York

Dollar Steamship Line, San Francisco
Dominion Line, Liverpool (British &
North Atlantic Steam Navigation
Company)
Donaldson Atlantic Line, Glasgow

ELMA (Empresa Lineas Maritimas
Argentinas), Buenos Aires
East Asiatic Co, Copenhagen (Det Ost-
asiatiske Kompagni Aktieselskabet)
East & West SS Co, Karachi
Eastern & Australian SS Co, London
Eastern Steam Navigation Co, Liverpool
**Efthycyprus Nav Co, Famagusta**
**C.S. Efthymiadis, Piraeus**
Egyptian Mail Steamship Co Ltd,
London
Elder Dempster & Co Ltd, Liverpool
Ellerman Lines Ltd, London (Ellerman
& Bucknall Steamship Co/The City
Line Ltd)
Epirotiki Lines SA, Piraeus
Europa-Canada Linie, Bremen

**Fairweather International Corporation,**
**Panama**
**Fearnley & Eger, Oslo**
Federal Steam Nav Co, London
**Finnlines O/Y, Helsinki**
**Finska Anfartygs A/B, Helsinki**
**Flagship Cruises Ltd, Monrovia**
Flota Argentina de Navegacion de
Ultramar, Buenos Aires
Flota Mercante del Estado, Buenos
Aires
Fratelli Grimaldi, Genoa
Freeport Cruise Inc, Monrovia
Furness, Withy & Co, London

Gdynia-America Line, Gdynia
Grace Line Inc, New York
Great Northern Steamship Co, New
York
Great Ship Co, London
**Greek Line, Piraeus (General Steam**
**Navigation Company of Greece)**
Grosvenor Shipping Co, Hong Kong

Hamburg-Amerika Linie, Hamburg
(Hapag; Hamburg-Amerikanische
Packetfahrt-AG)
Hamburg-Atlantik Linie, Hamburg
Hamburg-Süd, Hamburg (Hamburg-
Südamerikanische
Dampfschifffahrts-Gesellschaft)
**Hapag-Lloyd AG, Hamburg and**
**Bremen**

Hawaiian Steamship Co, New York
(Textron Inc)
Holland Afrika Lijn, The Hague
(VNSM; Vereenigde Nederlandsche
Scheepvaartmaatschappij, NV)
**Holland-Amerika Lijn, Rotterdam**
**(Nederlandsch-Amerikaansche**
**Stoomvaart Maatschappij)**
**Home Lines Inc, Genoa**

Incres Steamship Co Ltd, London
Indra Line, Liverpool (T. B. Royden &
Co)
Imman & International Steamship Co,
Liverpool
'Italia' Flotta Riunite, Genoa
'Italia' SpA di Navigazione, Genoa

**A. Jahre, Oslo**
Jugoslavenski Lloyd ad, London

**M. A. Karageorgis, Piraeus**
Kie Hock Shipping Co, Hong Kong
**A. F. Klaveness & Co A/S, Oslo**
**Klosters Rederi A/S, Oslo**
Koninklijke Hollandsche Lloyd, NV tot
Voortzetting vd, Amsterdam
Koninklijke Java-China
Paketvaartlijnen NV, Amsterdam
Koninklijke Nederlandsche Stoomboot
Mij, Amsterdam
Koninklijke Paketvaart Mij,
Amsterdam
G. Kotzovilis

F. Laeisz, Hamburg
Lamport & Holt Line, Liverpool
John S. Latsis, Athens
F. Leyland & Co, Liverpool
**Lloyd Brasileiro, Rio de Janeiro**
Lloyd Sabaudo SA per Azioni, Genoa
**Lloyd Triestino, Soc di Navigazione,**
**Trieste**
**Ø. Lorentzen, Oslo**
Los Angeles SS Co Inc, Wilmington,
California

Marimina Shipping Co SA
Matson Navigation Co, San Francisco
(Oceanic Steamship Co Inc)
McIlwraith, McEacharn Ltd,
Melbourne
Melbourne Steamship Co, Melbourne
Messageries Maritimes, Compagnie
des, Paris

Michigan-Ohio Nav Co, Wilmington,
Delaware
**Mitsubishi Shintako Ginko KK, Tokyo**
**Mitsubishi Shoji Kaisha, Tokyo**
Mitsui-OSK Lines, Tokyo
**Mogul Line Ltd, Bombay**
Moore-McCormack Lines Inc,
New York
Munson Steamship Line, New York

NV My Transoceaan, Rotterdam
National Steam Navigation Company
Greece, Piraeus
**Naviera Aznar SA, Bilbao**
Navigazione Generale Italiana, Genoa
Navigazione Libera-Triestino SA,
Trieste
Nelson Steam Navigation Co Ltd,
London
New York-Naples Steamship Co,
New York
New Zealand Shipping Co Ltd, London
Nikon Sangyo Junko Mihonichi Kyokai,
Tokyo
**Nippon Enkai Car Ferry, Tokyo**
**Nippon Kosoku Ferry Co Ltd, Tokyo**
Nippon Yusen KK, Tokyo
**Noordzee Veerdiensten, Rotterdam**
A/S Nord Line, Copenhagen
Norddeutscher Lloyd, Bremen
**Norske Amerikalinje, Oslo**
**North Sea Ferries Ltd, Hull**
**Norwegian Cruiseships A/S, Oslo**
**Nouvelle Compagnie de Paquebots,**
**Marseille**

**Ocean Queen Corporation, Panama**
**F. Olsen Ltd, London and Oslo**
Orient Steam Navigation Co, London
**Orient Overseas Line, Taipee**
Osaka Shosen KK, Osaka
Oshima Unyu KK, Kagoshima

**P & O Line, London (Peninsular &**
**Oriental Steam Navigation Co)**
P & O Orient Line, London
P. T. Affan Raya Line, Djakarta
P. T. Maskapai Pelajaran 'Sang Saka'
Djakarta
P. T. Pelajaran Nasional Indonesia,
Djakarta
**P. T. Perusahaan Pelajaran 'Arafat',**
**Djakarta**
Pacific Far East Line Inc, San Francisco
Pacific Mail Steamship Co, New York
Pacific Steam Navigation Co, Liverpool
Pacific Transport Co, Panama

Pacific Union Line Ltd, Hong Kong
Pan-Islamic Steamship Co, Karachi
Panama Pacific Line, New York
Panama Railroad Co, New York
People's Republic of China, Canton
Philippine Mail Line, Manila
Philippine President Lines Inc, Manila
Polish Navigation Co, New York
Polish Ocean Lines, Gdynia
   (Polskie Linie Oceaniczne)
Port Line Ltd, London
Providencia Shipping Co, Panama
Prudential-Grace Lines Inc, New York

Red Star Line, Antwerp; Liverpool;
   New York; Hamburg (Société Ano-
   nyme de Navigation Belge
   Americaine)
Rederi A/B Svea, Stockholm
Rederiaktiebolaget Sverige-
   Nordamerika, Gothenburg
Rotterdamsche Lloyd, NV Koninklijke,
   Rotterdam
Royal Caribbean Cruise Line A/S, Oslo
Royal Mail Lines Ltd, London (Royal
   Mail Steam Packet Company Ltd)
Royal Viking Line A/S, Bergen

SGTM (Société Générale de Transports
   Maritimes), Marseille
Scottish Shire Line, London
Shaw, Savill & Albion Co Ltd, London
Shin Nihonkai Ferry Co Ltd, Otaru
Shun Cheong Steam Navigation Co Ltd,
   Liverpool
'Sicula Americana', Soc di Navigazione,
   Palermo
Sicula Oceanica SA, Palermo
A/S Sigline, Stavanger (Berge Sigval
   Bergesen)
Sitmar Line, Genoa (Società Italiana
   Transporti Marittimi)
I. M. Skaugen & Co, Oslo
SNMC (Société Nationale Maritime
   Corse-Méditeraneée), Marseille
Soc Empresas Maritimas SA, Panama
Sociedade Geral de Comércio
   Industria e Transportes, Lisbon
Società Italiana di Servizi Marittimi,
   Rome
Soc Maritime Anversoise, Antwerp
South African Marine Corp, Cape Town
Southern Ferries Ltd, London (P & O)
Sovereign Cruise Ships Ltd, Famagusta
States Marine Lines Inc, Savannah

Stockholms Rederi A/B Svea,
   Stockholm
Stoomvaart Mij 'Nederland' NV,
   Amsterdam
Sun Line Inc, Piraeus
Sunsarda SpA, Trieste
Svenska Amerika Linjen A/B,
   Gothenburg

Tagus Navigation Co SA, Lisbon
Teiheio Enkai Ferry KK, Nagoya
The Adelaide Steam Ship Co,
   Melbourne
The Shipping Corporation of India Ltd,
   Bombay
Tor Line A/B, Gothenburg
Toyo Kisen Kaisha, Tokyo
Toyo Yusen KK, Tokyo
Transoceanic SS Co Ltd, Karachi
'Transoceanica', Società Italian di
   Navigazione, Genoa
Travemünde-Trelleborg-Linie GmbH &
   Co, Hamburg
C. Y. Tung, Hong Kong
Turner, Brightman & Co, London
Typaldos Bros, Piraeus
G. D. Tyser & Co, London

USSR, Moscow
Union-Castle Mail Steamship Co Ltd,
   London
Union Steamship Co Ltd, Southampton
Union Steamship Co of New Zealand,
   Wellington
Unione Austriaca di Navigazione SA,
   Trieste
United American Lines, New York
United Baltic Corp, London
United States Lines Inc, New York
United States Mail Steamship Co,
   New York
Universal Line SA, Panama

VEB Deutsche Seereederei, Rostock
VNSM (Vereenigde Nederlandsche
   Scheepvaartmaatschappij NV),
   The Hague
Victoria SS Co, Monrovia
Vintero Corporation, New York

Wallenius Bremen GmbH, Bremen
Ward Line, New York (New York &
   Cuba Mail Steamship Co)
White Star Line, Liverpool (Oceanic
   Steam Navigation Co)

A. Wilhelmsen & Co, Oslo
World Wide Cruise SA, Panama

Yacimientos Petroliferos Fiscales,
   Buenos Aires
Ybarra y Cia, Seville

Zim Israel Navigation Co Ltd, Haifa

The following are those firms listed in alphabetical order which built the ships dealt with in the five volumes of this work. Firms still in existence under these titles are printed in heavy type. Following each title is the number of passenger ships of 10,000 GRT and over built by the firm and to the right of the following stroke, the total gross tonnage of these ships. For example: 5/83,725 indicates that the firm built five such ships with a total gross tonnage of 83,725.

**AG 'Weser', otherwise known as Deschimag AG 'Weser', Bremen; 8/178,411 (including Werk Seebeck, Bremerhaven; 3/42,703)**
**Aalborg Vaerft A/S, Aalborg; 2/24,000**
Ansaldo SpA, Genoa-Sestri Ponente and La Spezia (now Italcantieri SpA); 15/380,069
Sir W. G. Armstrong, Whitworth & Co, Newcastle (now Vickers Ltd); 4/62,303
**Arsenal de Brest, Brest; 3/43,387**
**Arsenal de Lorient, Lorient; 1/10,944**
**Ateliers et Chantiers de Dunkerque et Bordeaux (France-Gironde), Dunkirk; 1/17,986**
Ateliers et Chantiers de France, Société des, Dunkirk (now Ateliers et Chatiers de Dunkerque et Bordeaux); 5/72,481
Ateliers et Chantiers de la Loire, St Nazaire (now Dubigeon-Normandie); 15/181,359

Barclay, Curle & Co, Glasgow; 17/213,702
Bartram & Sons, Sunderland; 1/10,308
W. Beardmore & Co, Dalmuir; 11/186,562
Bethlehem-Fairfield Shipyard Inc, Baltimore, Md; 1/10,139
Bethlehem Shipbuilding Corporation, Sparrows Point, Md (now Bethlehem Steel Corporation, Shipbuilding Division); 13/196,412
Bethlehem Steel Company, Shipbuilding Division, Quincy and Alameda (now Bethlehem Steel Corporation, Shipbuilding Division); built at Quincy, 6/92,348; built at Alameda, 10/167,518

**Blohm & Voss, Hamburg (now Blohm + Voss AG); 40/741,360**
Bremer Vulkan, Vegesack; 7/92,066
John Brown & Co Ltd, Clydebank (now Upper Clyde Shipbuilders Ltd); 47/1,088,459
**Burmeister & Wain, Copenhagen (now Burmeister and Wain's Skybsbyggeri); 4/55,334**
Burntisland SB Co Ltd, Burntisland; 1/11,046

Caird & Co, Greenock; 10/117,004
**Caledon Shipbuilding & Engineering Co Ltd, Dundee (now Robb Caledon Shipbuilders Ltd); 3/30,670**
**Cammell Laird & Co (Shipbuilders & Engineers) Ltd, Birkenhead; 22/331,171**
Cantiere Navale Felszegi, Muggia; 1/12,219
Cantiere Navale Triestino, Monfalcone (subsequently Cantiere Riuniti dell'Adriatico); 3/60,477
Cantieri ed Officini Meridionali, Soc Italiana per Construzioni Navali & Meccaniche, Baia, 2/23,387
**Cantieri Navali de Tirrenio e Riuniti SpA, Riva Trigoso; 2/33,977**
Cantieri Riuniti dell'Adriatico, Monfalcone and Trieste (now Italcantiere SpA); built at Monfalcone, 9/221,695; built at Trieste 12/239,523; built at San Marco, 1/11,693
Chantiers et Ateliers de la Gironde, Bordeaux (now Ateliers et Chantiers de Dunkerque et Bordeaux); 5/64,172
Chantiers Navals de La Ciotat; see Constructions Navales
**Cockatoo Docks & Engineering Co Pty Ltd, Sydney; 1/12,037**
**John Cockerill SA, Hoboken (subsequently Cockerill-Ougrée SA; now Cockerill Yards Hoboken SA, NV); 15/207,079**
**Constructions Navales, Soc Provencale de, La Ciotat (now Chantiers Navals de La Ciotat); 12/150,200**
Wm. Cramp & Sons, Philadelphia; 5/66,010

**'De Schelde', NV, Koninklijke Mij, Vlissingen; 9/130,648**
de Provence, Chantier et Ateliers, SA, Port de Bouc; 2/23,068

Wm. Denny & Bros, Dumbarton; 6/65,131
Deschimag AG 'Weser'; see AG 'Wes
Deutsche Werft AG, Hamburg; 3/51,812
Sir Raylton Dixon & Co, Middlesborough on Tees; 1/10,117
**Dubigeon-Normandie, Nantes; 8/92,466**

Eastern Shipbuilding Corporation, New London, Conn; 2/41,316
Soc Española de Construccion Naval SA, Bilbao and Ferrol (now Astiller Españoles SA); 11/127,116
Cia Euskalduna de Constrecion y Reparacion de Buques, Bilbao (now Astilleros Españoles SA); 1/10,226

Fairfield Shipbuilding & Engineering Co Ltd, Glasgow (now Upper Clyde Shipbuilders); 33/479,810
Federal Shipbuilding & Dry Dock Co Kearny, NJ; 11/196,208
Fijenoord, NV Mij voor Scheeps-en Werktuigbouw, Rotterdam (now Wilton-Fijenoord); 1/16,981
**Flender Werft AG, Lübeck; 2/31,32(**
**Forges et Chantiers de la Mediterrané Bordeaux and La Seyne (now Constructions Navales et Industriell de la Mediterranée); built at Bordeaux, 6/82,559; built at La Seyne, 1/24,002**
Furness Shipbuilding Co Ltd, Haverto Hill-on-Tees (now Swan Hunter Ship builders Ltd, Haverton Hill Shipyard); 1/10,699

Germaniawerft, Fried Krupp, AG, Kiel; 1/11,626
Gironde; see Chantiers et Ateliers de la Gironde
**AB Götaverken, Gothenburg; 2/23,37**

**Harland & Wolff, Belfast, Govan and Greenock (now Harland & Wolff Ltd); built at Belfast, 143/2,409,217 built at Govan 5/70,544; built at Greenock, 6/82,932**
R. & W. Hawthorn, Leslie & Co Ltd, Hebburn, Newcastle upon Tyne (now Swan Hunter Shipbuilders Ltd); 7/93,673
**Hayashikane Shosen KK, Shimonoseki; 1/12,000**

). & W. Henderson & Co, Glasgow;
1/10,963

Howaldtswerke AG, Kiel and Hamburg
(now Howaldtswerke-Deutsche Werft
AG); built at Kiel, 2/22,686; built at
Hamburg, 1/27,288

Ingalls SB Corporation, Pascagoula,
Miss; 9/108,560

Kaiser Company Inc, Richmond and
Vancouver; built at Richmond
42/468,660; built at Vancouver,
3/37,260

Kanasashi Zosensho, Shimizu;
1/12,529

Kanda Zosensho KK, Kure; 1/12,000

Kawasaki Dockyard Co Ltd, Kobe (now
Kawasaki Heavy Industries Ltd);
4/61,056

Kurushima Dock Co, Imabari;
3/35,420

LMG, Orenstein Koppel & Lübecker
Maschinenbau AG; 1/10,488

Sir James Laing, Sunderland (now
Doxford & Sunderland Ltd);
1/10,606

Lithgows Ltd, Port Glasgow (now
Lithgows [1969] Ltd); 2/21,834

London & Glasgow Engineering & Iron
Shipbuilding Co Ltd, Govan;
1/12,129

Mathias-Thesen-Werft VEB, Wismar;
5/98,709

Mitsubishi Dockyard Co, Nagasaki and
Kobe (now Mitsubishi Heavy
Industries Ltd); built at Nagasaki,
24/321,685; built at Kobe,
4/46,667; built at Shimonoseki,
1/10,223

Nakai Zosen KK, Setoda; 2/22,600

Nakskov Skibsvaerft Aktieselskabet,
Nakskov; 2/22,500

Napier & Miller Ltd, Glasgow;
2/21,852

NV Nederlandsche Scheepsbouw Mij,
Amsterdam (now Nederlandsche Dok
& Scheepsbouw Mij VoF);
12/168,891

The New York Shipbuilding Corporation, Camden, NJ; 25/338,069

Newport News Shipbuilding and Dry
Dock Co, Newport News, Va;
15/289,862

Nobiskrug GmbH, Rendsburg;
3/35,556

Nordseewerke, Rheinstahl, GmbH,
Emden; 2/39,810

Osaka Iron Works, Osaka (now Hitachi
Zosen); 1/11,616

Palmers Shipbuilding & Iron Co Ltd,
Jarrow (now Palmers Hebburn Co
Ltd, part of the Vickers group);
2/22,091

Penhoët, Chantiers et Ateliers de Saint-
Nazaire SA (now Chantiers de
L'Atlantique, Penhoët-Loire);
27/606,421

Reiherstieg Schiffswerfte und
Maschinenfabrik, Hamburg (now
Howaldtswerke-Deutsche Werft
AG); 1/10,056

Rotterdamsche Droogdok Mij NV,
Rotterdam; 3/84,976

Saint John Shipbuilding and Dry Dock
Co Ltd; 1/10,109

F. Schichau, Danzig; 7/129,833

Scott's Shipbuilding & Engineering Co
Ltd, Greenock (now Scott's Shipbuilding Co [1969] Ltd); 11/131,069

J. Scott, Russell & Co, Millwall,
London; 1/18,915

Seattle-Tacoma Shipbuilding Corp,
Tacoma, Wash.; 5/62,735

P. Smit jr, Rotterdam (now P. Smit jr
BV, Machinefabriek en Scheepswerf
van); 7/79,122

Soc Esercizio Bacini, Riva Trigoso
(now Cantieri Navali del Tirreno e
Riuniti SpA); 1/11,398

'Split' Brodogradiliste I Tvornika Dizel
Motora, Split; 1/10,451

Stabilimento Technico Triestino,
Trieste (now Italcantieri SpA);
1/25,661

A. Stephen & Sons, Glasgow (now
Upper Clyde Shipbuilders Ltd);
23/308,537

Sun Shipbuilding & Dry Dock Co,
Chester, Pa; 5/61,347

C. S. Swan & Hunter, Wallsend,
Newcastle-on-Tyne (now Swan
Hunter Shipbuilders Ltd); 4/48,667

Swan, Hunter & Wigham Richardson
Ltd, Newcastle; 23/338,527 (now
Swan Hunter Shipbuilders Ltd);
1/31,313

Tama Zosensho KK, Tama (now Mitsui
Zosen KK); 3/31,313

Joh. C. Tecklenborg AG, Geestemünde;
3/47,330

J. & G. Thomson, Glasgow (now Upper
Clyde Shipbuilders Ltd); 2/20,898

'Uljanik' Brodogradiliste, Pula;
1/10,444

Union Naval de Levante SA,
Astilleros de Valencia, Barcelona and
Valencia; 4/46,000

Upper Clyde Shipbuilders Ltd, Glasgow
and Clydebank; 1/10,420

Uraga Dock Co, Yokosuka (now
Sumimoto Shipbuilding and
Machinery Co Ltd, Uraga Ship-
building Yard); 1/10,343

C. van der Giessen & Zonen's,
Scheepswerven, NV, Krimpen a/d
Ijssel; 1/11,540

Vickers Ltd, Barrow-in-Furness (subsequently Vickers-Armstrongs);
8/134,873

Vickers Ltd, Barrow Shipbuilding
Works, Barrown-in-Furness &
Newcastle; 1/12,500

Vickers-Armstrongs Ltd, Barrow and
Newcastle; built at Barrow,
23/478,632; built at Newcastle,
10/189,187

'Vulcan', Stettiner Maschinenbau
Actien Gesellschaft, Stettin and
Hamburg; built at Stettin,
18/271,716; built at Hamburg,
4/98,126

Wärtsilä A/B, O/Y, Helsinki and
Turku; built at Helsinki, 7/143,997;
built at Turku 6/83,155

Western Pipe & Steel Co of California,
South San Francisco, Cal; 2/27,172

NV Wilton's Machinefabriek &
Scheepswerf, Schiedam (now Wilton-
Fijenoord Dok- en Werf Maats, NV);
2/20,375

Wilton-Fijenoord Dok- en Werf Maats.
NV, Rotterdam and Schiedam;
9/125,796

Workman, Clark & Co Ltd, Belfast;
24/277,936

Yokohama Dock Co, Yokohama;
3/40,742

# Bibliography and Acknowledgements

## Periodicals

Germanischer Lloyd, Register (Berlin, Hamburg) from 1899
Jane's Fighting Ships (London) from 1938
Lloyd's Register of Shipping (London) from 1888
Weyer's Taschenbuch der Kriegsflotten (Munich) from 1905

## Magazines

Die Seekiste (Kiel) 1950-1964
Engineering (London) 1888-1939
Fairplay (London) 1913-1919; 1972-1976
Hansa (Hamburg) 1950-1974
International Marine Engineering (New York) 1899-1935
Marine News (Kendall) 1950-1977
Motorship (New York) 1921-1932
Schiff und Hafen (Hamburg) 1952-1977
Schiffbau (Berlin) 1900-1939
Sea Breezes (Liverpool) 1949-1977
Shipbuilding and Shipping Record (London) 1918-1974
The Belgian Shiplover (Brussels) 1959-1975
The Marine Engineer (London) 1890-1914
The Motor Ship (London) 1924-1977
The Shipbuilder (London and Newcastle) 1906-1965
Zeitschrift des Vereins deutscher Ingenieure (Berlin) 1895-1914

## Books

Anderson, *White Star* (Prescot) 1964
Bonsor, *North Atlantic Seaway* (Prescot) 1955
de Boer, *The Centenary of the Stoomvaart Maatschappij 'Nederland' 1870-1970* (Kendal) 1970
*Dictionary of American Naval Fighting Ships* (Washington) Vol. I-IV
Dunn, *Passenger Liners* (Southampton) 1961
Dunn, *Famous Liners of the Past, Belfast Built* (London) 1964
Emmons, *Pacific Liners 1927-1972* (Newton Abbot) 1973
Farquhar, *Union Fleet 1875-1968* (Dunedin) 1968
Frick, *Passagierschiffe und*

*Autofähren der Welt* (Zurich and Stuttgart) 1967
Gröner, *Die deutschen Kriegsschiffe 1815-1945* (Munich) 1966
Hocking, *Dictionary of Disasters at Sea during the Age of Steam* (London) 1969
Hümmelchen, *Handelsstörer* (Munich) 1967
Isherwood, *Steamers of the Past* (Liverpool)
Jentschura-Jung-Mickel, *Die Japanischen Kriegsschiffe 1869-1945* (Munich) 1970
Kludas, *Die grossen deutschen Passagierschiffe* (Oldenburg and Hamburg) 1971
Le Fleming, *Blue Funnel Line* (Southampton) 1961
Maber, *North Star to Southern Cross* (Prescot) 1967
Michelsen, *Der U-Boots-Krieg 1914-1918* (Leipzig) 1925
Musk, *Canadian Pacific* (London) 1968
Overzier, *Der Amerikanisch-Englische Schiffahrtstrust* (Berlin) 1912
Rohwer, *Die U-Boot-Erfolge der Achsenmächte 1939-1945* (Munich) 1968
Rohwer-Hümmelchen, *Chronik des Seekrieges 1939-1945* (Oldenburg and Hamburg) 1968
Smith, *Passenger Ships of the World* (Boston) 1963
Worker, *The World's Passenger Ships* (London) 1967

## Other sources

Archives and publications of shipyards and shipping lines; statements and reports in newspapers.

I should like to register my very sincere thanks for the kind loan of photographs. The pictures in this book were obtained from the following sources:

AG 'Weser', Werk Seebeck, Bremerhaven, page 192
Angfartygs A/B Bore, Åbo, page 198
Marius Bar, Toulon, page 65/4
Bartram & Sons, Sunderland, page 158
A. Borchert, Hamburg, page 201/1
P.C. Brandwijk, Maassluis, pages 115/2, 117/3, 118/4, 146/2, 166/1
F.O. Braynard, Sea Cliff NY, pages 75/3, 136, 137/2, 139/4 & 5
Canadian Pacific Steamships Ltd, London, pages 96, 97/3, 98, 99/6, 182
Cia Trasatlantica Espanola SA, Madrid, page 43/3 & 4
Cie Générale Transatlantique, Paris pages 48/1, 49/2, 131
Cie Maritime Belge, Antwerp, page 104
Cunard Steam-Ship Co Ltd, London, pages 2, 87/4 & 5
Det Forenede D/S, Copenhagen, page 189/2
Dubigeon-Normandie, Nantes, page 177/2
A. Duncan, Gravesend, pages 26, 31/3, 41, 42/2, 51/2, 58/7, 71/2 & 4, 83/2, 85/3, 97/4, 107/2, 135/2, 149/3, 167
L. Dunn, Richmond, pages 55/3, 85/1 89/2, 101/2, 117/2, 135/1, 150/4, 161/1
R.K. Elber, Binningen, pages 103/3, 140/1, 141/2
Epirotiki Lines, Piraeus, page 37/3
Fir Line, Hongkong, pages 59/8, 61/12
C. Frick, Küsnacht, pages 55/4, 59/10, 137/3, 163/2
H. Graf, Hamburg, pages 25/3, 29/1, 51/1, 57/5, 87/6
Hapag-Lloyd AG, Hamburg and Bremen, page 79/2
H. Hartz, Hamburg, page 177/3
L. Höegh & Co A/S, Oslo, page 123/2
Home Lines, Genoa, page 147
Y. Ikeda, Osaka, pages 196/1, 199/4
'Italia' SAN, Genoa, pages 8, 9, 11/4, 12, 65/5, 142/1, 143/2 & 3
R. Izawa, Yokohama, pages 145/3, 184/3, 185/2
C. Jansen, Hamburg, pages 199/2 & 3, 201/2
M.A. Karageorgis, Piraeus, page 69/4
Kawasaki Heavy Industries, Ltd, Kobe, page 183
R. Kleyn, Voorburg, pages 21/2, 27/3, 31/2, 36, 39/3, 47/4, 52, 76/5, 81/4, 88/1, 89/3, 93/2, 105/3, 107/3 108, 121/1, 124/4, 125/6, 129/2, 150/5, 157/2, 179/2 & 3
Klosters Rederi A/S, Oslo, pages 168 169/2 & 3

K.P. Lewis, Bromborough, page
191/3
Lloyd Triestino, Trieste, pages 13, 14,
15/3 & 4, 17/5 & 6, 19/7 & 8, 132,
133
J.G.B. Lovie, Wellington, pages 27/2,
57/6, 77/7, 78/8, 99/7, 115/3, 121/2,
125/5, 129/3, 130/1 & 2, 151/1, 159
H.J. Mayburg, Bremen, page 79/1
Messageries Maritimes, Marseille,
pages 53, 54, 59/9, 60, 61/13 & 14
F. van Otterdijk, Hoboken, pages
23/1, 186/1 & 2
Peninsular and Oriental Steam
Navigation Co, London, pages 23/2,
176, 178
J.F. van Puyvelde, Brussels, pages
46/3, 63/3, 71/3, 77/6, 82, 83/1, 111,
153/2, 162/1, 173
H.-J. Reinecke, Hamburg, pages
39/4, 73/1, 85/2, 93/3, 103/2, 110
Rheinstahl Nordseewerke GmbH,
Emden, pages 174, 175/2 & 3
Royal Mail Lines Ltd, London, page
122/1
Shaw, Savill & Albion Co Ltd, London
pages 90/1, 91/2
Skyfotos, Ashford Airport, Kent,
pages 25/4, 35/2, 128
P. Smit jr BV, Rotterdam, page 40
Travemünde-Trelleborg-Line GmbH
& Co, Hamburg, page 195/1
Uglands Rederi A/S, Grimstad, page
123/2
Union-Castle Main Steamship Co Ltd,
London, pages 44, 45/2, 47/5, 95, 113
Union Naval de Levante SA,
Barcelona and Valenica, pages 187/1
& 2, 190, 191/2
Uraga Dock Co, Yokosuka, page 134
Vickers Ltd, Barrow-in-Furness, page
189/1
Wärtsilä A/B, O/Y, Helsinki and
Turku, pages 170, 171/2 & 3, 180,
181/2 & 3, 202/1, 203/2 & 3, 206/1
Werft Nobiskrug, Rendsburg, page
205/2
World Ship Society, F.R. Sherlock,
Southampton, page 193/2

All other photographs are from the
author's collection.

This index includes all ships whose names appear in Volumes 1-5. The Roman numeral preceding the page number denotes the particular volume in which the reference appears.